Chickens and How To Raise Them

All About Chickens, How To Hatch, House, Feed and Fatten Them

by A.T. Johnson

with an introduction by Jackson Chambers

This work contains material that was originally published in 1910.

This publication is within the Public Domain.

*This edition is reprinted for educational purposes
and in accordance with all applicable Federal Laws.*

Introduction

I am pleased to present yet another title on Poultry.

This volume is entitled "Chickens and How To Raise Them" and was published by A.T. Johnson in 1910.

The work is in the Public Domain and is re-printed here in accordance with Federal Laws.

As with all reprinted books of this age that are intended to perfectly reproduce the original edition, considerable pains and effort had to be undertaken to correct fading and sometimes outright damage to existing proofs of this title. At times, this task is quite monumental, requiring an almost total "rebuilding" of some pages from digital proofs of multiple copies. Despite this, imperfections still sometimes exist in the final proof and may detract from the visual appearance of the text.

I hope you enjoy reading this book as much as I enjoyed making it available to readers again.

Jackson Chambers

Kellerstrass Farm
Arthur Oscar Schilling
1907

1

2

PREFACE

In the following pages the author deals in a systematic and thorough way with the subjects of natural and artificial incubation, and the rearing of chickens. He commences with a chapter on Nature's method of incubation, then fully describes the wonderful structure of an egg, following with chapters on the development of the embryo, the importance of securing good eggs for incubation, incubation by the hen and by artificial means; the merits and otherwise of moist and non-moisture incubators and their management, the rearing of chickens by natural and artificial means, weaning and feeding the chickens, rearing in winter; concluding with some sound useful advice regarding various common ailments in chickens.

INDEX

CHICKENS
And How to Raise Them

CHAPTER I

PREFATORY NOTES FROM NATURE

To enable him to thoroughly grasp the somewhat complex subject of incubation, the student would do well to briefly consider the different processes which Nature adopts for the safety of the embryo young during its development. All animals begin life within an egg. If we consider first the fishes, we find the female depositing her eggs in the water, when they are left to take their chance of being fertilized by the medium which is also deposited in the water by the male. These eggs are exposed to many dangers, but in the countless numbers that one fish will yield the safety of the species against extermination is guaranteed. When we come to reptiles, their eggs are discovered to be fertilized before they leave the body of the mother, and, compared with those of fishes, are few in number. They are fewer in number because the offspring have a better chance of surviving than the young of fishes, and because the eggs themselves are protected either by the parent or by some other provision of nature. The next step from the reptile is the bird, and here we find a great stride made in the history of evolution. Not only are the eggs of a bird beautifully adapted for the purpose for which they are formed, but over them the female, and often the male, extends a solicitous care. The rudiments of all those higher attributes which characterize the instincts and emotions of the mammalia—of man himself—we may see in bird life. And in the embryo's development within the egg we can read the story of the evolution of living creatures.

In birds, as we shall see, the warmth of the mother's body, which is necessary for the growth of the embryo, is bestowed from her breast as she " sits " upon the eggs. On the other hand, in mammalia the egg, or the germ of life which is contained in an egg-form, is fertilized and developed within the body of the mother, and brought forth in due time as a little reproduction of herself.

Here, however, we are mainly concerned with bird life, and turning again to Nature as a guide, in the matter of incubation particularly, what do we find? Many object lessons of value, many which are complex and hard to understand. Nests for the reception of birds' eggs are made of every conceivable shape and form, or they are not made at all, the eggs being merely deposited on a bare slab of rock. The Long-tailed Tit and the Wren often choose the most sheltered sites for their nests, and build them domed, of the warmest material, and of great thickness. A thin, airy platform of twigs high up on some naked bough is all that the Wood Pigeon makes for her nest and nursery. There are nests far down in a deep, dark hole of a tree, or swinging in a frail basket-work of grass and twigs at the end of a bough. The Ostrich hens scrape a large hole in the sand with their feet, and in it a great number of eggs are deposited —not by one bird, but by the whole colony. Much of the heat necessary for incubation in this case is provided by the sun-warmed sand, but the cock bird sits upon the "nest" by night, the hens protecting it by day from prowling enemies.

The most interesting form of incubation is that adopted by the Megapodes, or mound-building turkeys, of the Celebes. These birds collect together huge mounds of leaves, earth, and decaying substances, which are often fifteen to twenty feet high, and thirty to a hundred feet in circumference. The materials of which these mounds are made soon begin to ferment, and so engender heat, which lasts a considerable time, particularly as the pile is frequently being added to by its owners. For many miles round the Megapodes congregate together for the building of this natural incubator, and in it they deposit eggs in large numbers. In course of time the eggs hatch, without any attention whatever having been bestowed upon them after laying by the parent birds. The young are left entirely to themselves, and, unlike those of any other known species, are able to fly and seek food immediately after birth !

Now what deductions can be made from the foregoing observations ? The nest is, in the first place, a receptacle for the eggs undergoing incubation, and, generally speaking, a home for the young until they are old enough to leave their parents, or to go away with the latter in search of food. That eggs do not require a nest constructed of any definite material, or placed in any particular site, for their successful development is equally true. The majority of them are, however, airy structures, the peculiar, almost fantastic forms of many of them being the result of natural selection working for the protection of the species, and to some extent the birds' æsthetic sense may be responsible. But the fact that birds' eggs hatch so successfully under so many diverse conditions goes far toward assisting us in unraveling the knot that for so long has kept the subject of incubation in mystery. All birds' eggs are alike, made of the same materials or ingredients. They all develop under the influence of a proper warmth. They differ only in the length of time which development occupies, and in the conditions under which they exist during that period. Hidden in these facts are the fundamental principles upon which our practice of modern incubation has been built.

CHAPTER II

THE STRUCTURE OF AN EGG

BEFORE one can possibly become proficient in the subject of practical incubation he must be conversant with the formation of an egg. It should be scarcely necessary to remark that, although an egg is an important and nutritious article of food, Nature never intended it for that purpose. It has been designed not only as the most suitable receptacle for the embryo life of a bird, but its whole contents are especially and beautifully adapted for the requirements of that embryo during the imprisoned period of its early career. The egg, to the tiny germ which it contains, is as a mother who gives to her helpless offspring not only protection but sustenance and material for growth. That fact the student of incubation must bear in mind.

The Ovary.—If a hen during her laying period were to be examined internally one would find attached to the spine a cluster of globular objects, called the ovary (A, Fig. 1). The largest of these are like an ordinary yolk of an egg, and they hang at the bottom of the bunch. Those nearer the spine are smaller. In fact, we should find these round objects, which are yolks in various stages of development, of all sizes from the largest, which are more than an inch in diameter, to the smallest ones at the root of the cluster, which are scarcely visible to the naked eye. Every day, or more commonly every other day, one of these larger yolks comes to maturity ; and, whether fertilization has taken place or not, breaks away from the tiny bag which contained it, called the "ovisac," and enters the wide mouth (B, Fig. 1) of the egg-passage, or "oviduct." When it is received into the oviduct it is enclosed in a thin membrane, and, as it passes along, those other portions which go to make it a perfect egg are secreted and formed.

Albumen, or " White."—The first of these is the albumen, or " white." This clothes the yolk in layers (which can be readily seen if a hard-boiled egg be cut across in slices) as it passes along the oviduct. Its uses are various, and it is of the utmost importance to the embryo chick. It protects the delicate germ from sudden shocks and extremes of temperature, and forms the main nourishment upon which the embryo lives and grows during the period of incubation.

The Air Cell.—When the egg has received the albumen it becomes entirely surrounded with two membranes, or skins, which lie immediately under the shell. At the larger end of the egg these membranes separate, forming a space known as the air cell (AC, Fig. 2). In the fresh egg this chamber is very small, but as time goes on, and the contents of the egg evaporate (the albumen contains about seventy-eight per cent. of water in its composition), it becomes considerably larger. During incubation, too, it increases in size, often occupying over one-fifth of the entire egg as the latter approaches the date of hatching.

The Shell.—The last thing with which the egg is invested is the shell, which is formed of a limy material secreted by the walls of the oviduct. This shell, or outer covering, being designed by Nature to protect the contents of the egg, is enormously strong for its thickness and peculiar formation. Yet it is so made that the particles of lime admit of a free passage of air between them. It is porous, so that the embryo within, as we shall see later, can breathe the outer air.

Fig. 1.—THE OVARY OR EGG ORGANS OF A HEN
References : A, Ovary ; B, Oviduct ; c, Egg in the Duct

One more remarkable fact may be mentioned here with regard to the shell. It is often a puzzle to many people how such a frail creature as

an unborn chicken can break itself out of its
prison walls, and it is no doubt a cause for
wonder. But we must bear in mind that the
shell of a fresh egg and that of one on the point
of hatching are two very different things. While
incubation is going on, a softening of the shell is
also progressing. By means of the chemical
changes which take place as the embryo breathes,
the particles of lime undergo a change, and become disintegrated, so that by the time the
chicken is ready to hatch, the shell is comparatively easily broken. Thus Nature, economical
always, has made one purpose serve another.
Fig. 1, C, shows the egg passing along the oviduct
just before expulsion.

The Chalazæ.—Most people know what an egg
looks like when it is broken into a saucer. In
the middle is the yolk (Fig. 2, y), and around it
the albumen (w). At each side of the former
may be seen a twisted and rather more dense
portion of albumen, whiter than the rest. These
chalazæ (Fig. 2, ch), as they are called, have nothing directly to do with the germ, as many people
suppose. They consist, as we have already said,
of denser albumen, and are, in a mechanical way,

of the utmost importance. They act as buffers
to prevent the yolk from being injured by a sudden jar, and, being attached as they are on opposite sides and a little below the yolk, serve as
balances, which always keep the latter in the
same relative position. It does not matter how
much an egg may be turned round, the chalazæ
prevent the yolk from turning with it, holding
it always with the germ uppermost.

The Germ Spot, or Blastoderm.—If the yolk of
a hard-boiled egg be cut in two, it will be seen
that the central and upper part is of a paler
color than the remainder. The former is known
as the white yolk (Fig. 2, *wy*), the latter as the
yellow (Fig. 2, *y*). It is on the surface of the
white yolk that the germ of the egg rests.
Turning again to the broken egg in the saucer, we
shall see on the uppermost surface of the yolk a
tiny disc, or ring, about one-eighth of an inch in
diameter. This is the germ-spot (Fig. 2, *gs*), or
blastoderm (Gr. blastos—a sprout, and derma—a
skin). Whether the egg be fertile or not this
disc is always present, and proof of fecundation
having taken place can only be ascertained with
the aid of a lens. It is from the centre of the

germ-spot that the development of the chicken begins. From an invisible speck, hidden there, the embryo will grow, and, under proper conditions, absorbing the whole of the contents of the egg, emerge in three weeks a perfect chicken.

Soft or Shell-less Eggs.—Having briefly traced the origin and formation of an egg, the beginner

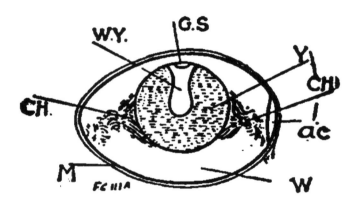

Fig. 2.—SECTION OF AN EGG

References: Membrane; C H, Chalazæ; W Y, White Yolk; G S, Germ Spot; Y, Yellow Yolk; A C, Air Cell; W, White or Albumen

will now be better able to understand why hens sometimes lay abnormal eggs. For instance, it is not difficult to comprehend how, in a hen whose ovary is very prolific, two yolks may become detached, and enter the oviduct together, with the result that a "double-yolked egg" is laid. Or we can see how a hen whose organs of reproduction are unduly stimulated might produce eggs and lay them faster than the oviduct can shell them. They are what are generally called "soft," or "shell-less" eggs, and may either be enclosed in the membrane only or have shells of a very thin texture. Again, a hen will sometimes lay yolks only, no abumen or lime having been secreted by the oviduct, but such instances are more uncommon, and of more serious consequence. In any case, even if the shell only appears abnormal, such eggs are seldom fertile.

CHAPTER III

THE DEVELOPMENT OF THE EMBRYO

IF we look back through the story of the embryo's growth to the very beginning, it is as if we saw an epitome of the evolution of animal life upon the earth. From the single cell—from which all organisms are supposed to have developed—we can trace the development of a creature until its final stage is completed, and it is able to move about and reproduce its kind.

Genesis of Life.—The germinal disc which, as we have already said, rests upon the upper surface of the yolk, may at its earliest stage be compared with the ovule of a plant, which remains inactive until a little grain of pollen unites with it. Then, as we all know, the union of these two—the pollen and the ovule, the father and the mother—produces a young plant which is the joint product of its two parents. In like manner the germ of an egg as it enters the oviduct is a single cell, but as it passes along, and fecundation takes place, it divides and subdivides into a being consisting of many cells. That is to say, life has commenced. What it is that endows the tiny creature with life and movement; what power it is that first creates the faint wave-like motion of the primitive heart, we do not know. It is one of the deepest mysteries in Nature, and one that need not be further discussed in a volume of this kind.

Egg, a Delicate Living Organism.—It will now be understood that before an egg is laid, provided it be fertile, the life of the minute embryo has already gone through several stages. It has started on its life's journey, but when the egg becomes cold, after it has been laid, the embryo lapses into a quiescent condition, in which it remains until warmth is restored, when growth is again resumed. At the same time this germ, inactive and torpid as it appears to be, is a frail and delicate organism, very susceptible to extremes of temperature and rough usage. The longer an egg is kept before being incubated the weaker the germ becomes; the fresher the egg the stronger the embryo. At any time during incubation an embryo may die through sheer inability to live, having inherited weakness from its parents; or it may succumb to sudden concussions or loud noises. The student of incubation should therefore train himself to look upon every fertile egg, not only before incubation but during the process, as a living organism of great delicacy, that requires gentle handling. It would serve no useful purpose in a work of this

Fig. 3.—First Signs of Life in a Germinating Egg

kind to follow in all its minute detail the development of the embryo during incubation, but a glance at the principal stages of its growth will be of great assistance in helping the beginner to better understand the subject of incubation, whether natural or artificial.

First Stages of Germination.—After a hen's egg has been subjected to the proper temperature

—say 104 degrees—for a few hours the germ-spot (Fig. 3) enlarges and elongates. It is lying in a slight hollow on the surface of the yolk, and in about forty-eight hours the little network of blood-vessels, which are spreading out from the central spot like the fibrous roots of a tree, begin to pulsate with the movement of the blood. At this stage the embryo is surrounded by a trans-

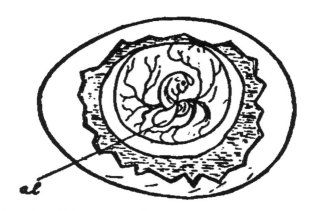

Fig. 4.—Embryo About the Fifth Day
Reference: AL, Allantois

parent sac, called the " amnion," but no sooner does the circulation of the blood begin than another organ of the greatest importance is developed. This is the "allantois" (Fig. 4). It is a semi-transparent sac or bag, that, starting from the navel of the embryo, gradually increases in size until it entirely surrounds the contents of the egg, its extremities coming in contact with the shell. This organ is furnished with a system of blood-vessels, and serves as a lung for the embyro. It oxygenates the blood, purifies it by bringing it in contact with the oxygen of the air which passes through the shell, and returns it revived to the heart. Thus we can readily understand how important it is to keep the egg shells clean during incubation, so that their porosity be not obstructed in any way. We can understand, too, the necessity for fresh air in the incubator and incubator room. If the pores of an egg's shell were to be closed up the embryo would die of suffocation, just as we should do if we were shut up in a sealed chamber and deprived of the life-giving, purifying oxygen of fresh air.

Development of Wings, Legs, and Feathers.— During the growth of the allantois, little rudiments of wings and legs have appeared as sprouts upon the inner side of the embryo (Fig. 4). At the tenth or eleventh day some rudiments of feathers begin to show, and the bony skeleton is in process of formation. All this time the chicken appears to have been subsisting upon the yolk, which, however, does not decrease in size.

The albumen, on the other hand, has considerably diminished, and the explanation appears to be that the yolk, connected as it is with the navel, or "umbilicus," serves as a medium through which the nutritive properties of the albumen are conveyed to the digestive canal of the chicken.

Final Stage of Development.—At the fourteenth or fifteenth day the embryo is nearly as long as the egg, and would be longer but for its curled-up position. Nature now endows it with her "finishing touches." The feather tracts become more noticeable, the toe-nails have appeared; the beak hardens, becomes more shapely, and a little limy point grows on its tip to assist the chicken in breaking its way through the shell. Some time during the nineteenth or twentieth day the chick pierces the membrane that covers it, and for the first time breathes the air (which is contained in the air cell already referred to, and which by this time is very much enlarged) with its true lungs. The blood ceases to flow into the allantois, which is required no longer, and the chicken, methodically removing the larger half of the shell by a chipping process, tumbles out, and tastes liberty for the **first** time.

Not only do the allantois and amnion almost entirely disappear during the hatching process, but what remains of the yolk is quickly drawn into the body of the chicken through the navel.

Thus Nature completes her wonderful story of development by providing the newly-born chicken with sufficient nourishment, in the form of the yolk, to sustain it for the first twenty-four hours, at least, of its life, after which it is well able to feed itself, provided food be within reach.

CHAPTER IV

EGGS FOR HATCHING

So much depends upon the selection of suitable eggs for incubation that a separate chapter may here be devoted to the subject.

Importance of Obtaining Good Eggs.—We have seen that a fertile egg is the joint product of its two parents, and, that being so, it—or, rather, the chicken which it produces—not only inherits an outward likeness to its father and mother, but an inward constitutional resemblance. In other words, sickly or immature stock birds will produce weak chickens, and vice versa. Most of the failures in incubation may be directly traced to the parents, which are in some way or another physically unfit. Immaturity in the stock birds is one of the most frequent causes of these failures, particularly when both the male and females are under age. Another source of disappointment in hatching may be found in disease. The breeding stock may be suffering from tuberculosis, or some such ailment, which will assuredly be passed on to the youngsters, if not in its original form in some other. There may not be any actual disease in the stock, but they are badly managed, with the result that vigor and strength have given way to lassitude and obesity, and this, again, is a fruitful cause of " dead in shell " or sickly chickens.

In-breeding.—In-breeding—the mating together of close relations, such as brothers and sisters— has been denounced as an evil practice, and rightly so in some respects, for, generally speaking, the offspring of in-bred parents is weaker constitutionally than the young of a male and female of different blood. But in-breeding in itself need not be directly harmful. It need not be the bogie that some people make it out to be. In the production of some of the finest races of our poultry in-breeding has been necessary, and we are accustomed to look only at the evil results and shut our eyes to the good. The truth about this much-discussed subject is, we think, something like this. All beings are subject to constitutional defects. Few, if any, are perfect. Then if we mate two animals which are of the same blood, and which by the laws of heredity will possess the same flaws in their respective constitutions, together we must expect to find those flaws intensified, made worse, in the off-spring. If, on the other hand, we mate two un-related animals, the chances are that they will not have defects in common, with the result that the young will, although inheriting, perhaps, some of the weaknesses (as well as the vigor) of either parent, not suffer from the combined effects of two defective parents. But supposing we were to have a brother and sister, say, of some robust breed like the Old English Game, which, so far as we could ascertain, were perfectly sound in a general sense, and we mated them together, we should expect the chickens to be as robust as the parents. Here in-breeding will have had no ill-effects, because there were no physical deformities or shortcomings common to the two sexes. It is only where there is constitutional taint on either side that in-breeding is harmful. Nature in-breeds continuously, but, be it remembered, how physically perfect are the beings she employs! Any constitutional flaw is wiped out with ruthless severity. She teaches "in-breeding," but "selection" also, and her pruning-knife is very sharp. We have gone into this part of the subject at some length because by a careful study of it the thoughtful student will gather much that will be useful to him in practical incubation.

Collecting and Storing Eggs for Incubation.— Eggs for hatching, or, indeed, for any purpose, ought to be collected at least once daily. In frosty weather twice a day is not too often. Sometimes it may be desired to store the eggs required for hatching for a week or so, but, as I have pointed out, the fresher the egg the better will it hatch. In storing, various ways have been tested, and much discussion has arisen as to whether they ought to be in a warm place or a cold one, and so on. In our experience the following is the best way. See that the eggs are clean, and pack them in boxes of bran, the latter stuffed around pretty tight. If they are placed on end, the large one for preference, the necessity for turning each day will be done away with. Keep the boxes in a dry place of moderate temperature and out of draughts, and the eggs will keep two or three weeks quite well ; but whether they will hatch so successfully as fresh ones is another matter. It depends a great deal on the strength of the germ. Whenever eggs are kept on their sides they must be turned over daily. No preservative of any kind may be applied to the shells. The bran will retard evaporation of the contents, and so prevent too great an enlargement of the air cell.

It is always desirable, in selecting eggs for hatching, to choose those which are of normal size and shape. Any with thin or malformed shells ought to be discarded, and used for table.

The Sex in Eggs a Fallacy.—Although there are a host of traditions regarding eggs for hatching, particularly on the subject of foretelling sex, they may all be ignored as entirely untrustworthy. Remarkable coincidences are recorded from time to time, but they have been as often refuted by practical experiment. Generally speaking, perhaps, there are more cockerels bred early in the year, and the male sex is more predominant in the offspring of very vigorous parents. No definite statements can, however, be made on the subject, except that to foretell sex in eggs is an impossibility.

Treatment of Eggs Received by Rail or Post.— When eggs for hatching have been traveling by rail or post, it is always desirable to unpack them and let them rest on their sides for twelve or eighteen hours before placing them in the incubator or under the hen. Whether the germ becomes " fatigued," or otherwise " upset " by the journey, cannot be ascertained, but it has been proved beyond a doubt that a " rest " revives it, and materially assists the hatching process.

A Final Word on the Subject.—Finally, in concluding this chapter, let us once more emphasize the importance of keeping one's stock birds robust and vigorous. The most skilful operator cannot hatch chickens successfully from weakly germs, the offspring of weakly parents. To the latter, as we have already said, most of the hatching failures can be traced. Too often the perplexed beginner who is worrying himself about moisture, ventilation, temperature, and such like, and perhaps calling the maker of the incubator hard names, may find the cause of failure in his own breeding-pens.

CHAPTER V

NATURAL INCUBATION: THE SITTING HEN

AFTER a hen has been laying for some time, and has completed her "batch" of eggs, she indicates a desire to sit by remaining on the nest

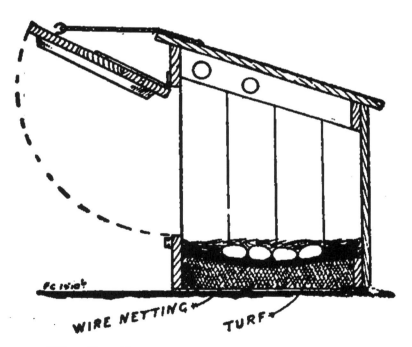

WIRE NETTING   TURF

Fig. 5.—SECTION OF A SITTING NEST

for considerable periods during the day, until at length she remains there altogether, coming off only at long intervals to feed. Such a hen will generally peck at a hand placed near her when

on the nest, the instinct of protecting her eggs
and young already beginning to assert itself, and
when at liberty she goes about with feathers
erect and " clucking " as if she were calling her
brood. Some hens become broody, or evince a
desire to sit, more often than others, and the

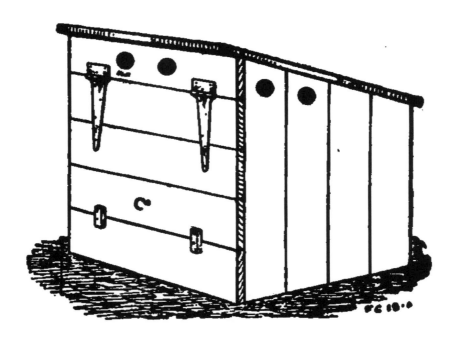

Fig. 6.—Sitting Nest Closed

Mediterranean breeds, through their being so
rigorously selected for eggs, have lost the brood-
ing instinct altogether. These are called non-
sitters, yet it seems somewhat strange—except
when viewed in the light of science—that the
union of two non-sitters, say a Houdan and a

Leghorn, will produce a cross-bred fowl which often makes an excellent sitter and mother.

The Best Broodies are those hens which are compact in shape, fairly full in plumage, with fine legs, and feet free from feathers. The Orpington or Wyandotte, in any variety, may be given as a good class. The heaviest hens are liable to crush the eggs entrusted to them, although for incubating goose or turkey eggs a Cochin, Brahma, or large Plymouth Rock cannot be excelled. Game hens make very good sitters, squatting closely, and covering more eggs than one would imagine possible. They are, too, careful mothers, and extraordinarily courageous in protecting their young. It is not an uncommon sight to see a Game hen, especially an Old English, attacking a cow or pig that happens to approach too close to her brood.

A Properly Constructed Nest is just as important as a good sitter (Figs. 5, 6, and 7). It is easily made, but that does not mean to say that it can be made anyhow, as some people appear to think. We may differ in the details of its construction, but there are certain unalterable rules which we must abide by. For example, the box in which it is to be made must be large enough—not less than eighteen inches each way. It must have a wire or lattice door at the front, some holes bored at the sides near the top, and a piece of wood about three inches deep nailed across the foot to prevent the material from falling out when the door is open. A floor is

Fig. 7.—Sitting Nest with a Wire Door

desirable as a protection against mice and rats. The interior should have a thorough dressing of limewash containing a little carbolic, and when this is dry the nest can be made. The box need not be waterproof, for it is best placed in a shed at a convenient height from the floor, and several may be put one upon the other in tiers, so long as the interiors of all are clearly visible to the attendant. Before the actual nesting material is used, a shovelful of garden soil must be placed at the bottom of the box, and worked into the corners with the hand until a saucer-shaped hollow is formed. This must neither be too deep nor too flat. If the former the outside eggs will roll down upon those in the centre, when they would probably be broken by the hen, and if it is not deep enough the eggs will spread about, and the sitter will be unable to cover them. Having made the foundation satisfactorily, and beaten the soil down fairly firm with the palm of the hand, some short, soft hay must be put upon it as a lining material. It requires a little practice to make the hay lie evenly and smooth, but if it is shaken lightly into its place, not much being used at a time, and then worked down by a circular motion of the hand, a firm, well shaped nest will be the result. Rather more hay should be used in winter and spring than in warm weather. , (See Fig. 8.)

Protecting Sitting Hens from Vermin.—Before the broody hen is put upon the nest she must be thoroughly drenched with insect-powder, getting

it well underneath the feathers. It is desirable
to do this even when there is no vermin visible;
and the nest should also be well dusted with the
powder. There is no doubt that thousands of
eggs are spoiled every year through the hen being irritated by insect vermin, and even if she
manages to hatch her eggs successfully, she
cannot rear the chickens when tormented by
these pests. It is scarcely possible to exaggerate
the extreme importance of keeping the sitting
hen free from vermin.

Placing a Sitting Hen on the Nest.—The best
time to place a broody upon the nest that has
been prepared for her is the evening. Some hens
are naturally more wild and excitable than
others, but even these will settle down more
composedly at dusk. Do not give the broody
the eggs which she is to sit upon until she has
become quite used to the nest, or she may break
them. Let her have half-a-dozen "pot" ones,
which are cheap enough, for the first day at
least. In the early months of the year, when
most of the hatching is done, it is a mistake to
give a hen a large "clutch." Nine or ten eggs
are as many as a medium-sized sitter can manage.

If she has more those on the outside may get
chilled, and as all the eggs are daily, at least,
moving their positions in the nest, the whole lot
may by the date of hatching become addled.
Again, it must be remembered that a hen cannot

Fig. 8.—A WELL-MADE NEST

take proper care of a large brood of chickens in
the colder months.

Management of the Sitting Hen.—Sitting hens
must always be handled gently. Once daily
they require feeding and exercise, and should be
lifted off their nests, care being taken that their

feet or wings do not drag any eggs out with them. Provide them with as much cracked maize as they care to eat, and a plentiful supply of water and grit. A dusting place must be prepared in one corner of the shed, and while the birds are feeding, dusting, and exercising an inspection of the nests should be made. If any have been fouled by the birds, or contain broken eggs, they should be relined, and the eggs thoroughly washed in tepid water. Sometimes the breast feathers of a hen who has smashed some of her eggs require washing also, or they will adhere to the eggs, causing another breakage when she is lifted off the following morning. During the first week of incubation the broodies may be allowed off for five or six minutes, but after that period has elapsed twice as long may be allowed them. A hen must always be allowed to pass her evacuations before she is replaced on the nest, or the latter will assuredly be fouled by the following day. Regularity in the hour of feeding each day should be strictly maintained, for if there is any delay some hens may get restless and cause breakages. Quietness is necessary in and about the sitting shed, and if the nests have open fronts a thick piece of sacking should be suspended across them by way of a blind.

Testing the Eggs on Ninth Day.—At about the

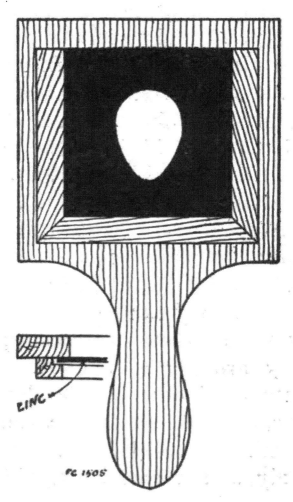

Fig. 9.—An Egg Tester
Diaphragms to suit the various sizes of eggs may easily be adjusted to the Tester

ninth day the eggs may be tested, and the unfertile ones picked out. Some people advise more frequent testing, but, in the case of natural incubation particularly, I do not consider it either necessary or desirable. The operation must be conducted at night, and all that is required is a candle and a piece of cardboard with a hole in it which is rather smaller than the egg (Fig. 9). An expert tester does not even require that. He simply takes the egg between the finger and thumb of his left hand, screening the light from his eyes with his right, and holds it before a candle, or, better still, a bull's-eye lantern. And for all general purposes this is enough. An unfertile egg will appear, when between the eye and the light, exactly like a fresh one. These should be sorted out and used either for the chickens or cooking purposes, for which they are perfectly good. Those eggs which contain chickens will be dark, approaching opacity, and the air cell at the larger end will be distinctly visible. An addled egg appears cloudy, and a dark spot, with perhaps a red streak near it, may be seen, as if adhering to the shell on one side. There will be no doubt about the unfertile, or " clear " eggs, but if the operator is uncertain as to any of the others he should mark them with a pencil, and test again in a week's time. It is during the early months of the year, when there are more unfertile eggs, or when there is any doubt as to the fecundity of the stock birds, that testing has its advantages. If two broody hens, for example, were to be set the same day, and half the eggs proved to be unfertile, the remainder might be given to one of the hens and the other reset with a fresh clutch. Addled eggs, again, if left in the nest emit poisonous gases, which can be anything but good for the living embryos, to which, as we have seen, fresh, pure air is so essential.

The Period of Hatching.—At the nineteenth day the sitting hen should not be lifted off the nest until it has been ascertained whether the eggs are beginning to "chip." This may be done by placing the hand under the bird's breast and gently raising her up. If none of the eggs shows signs of hatching she may be lifted off as usual, but if any are starred (see Fig. 10) she is best left alone, a small quantity of grain being placed within reach. All being well, the chickens should hatch from the twentieth to the twenty-first day, without any attention being bestowed

upon them by the attendant. In fact, the less he
has to do with them the better. Once, perhaps,
when he thinks the hatch is rather more than
half completed, he may gently slip his hand
under the hen and remove the empty shells, but
to be continually " having a peep " is not con-
ducive to the best results. It not infrequently
happens that some embryos fail, through weakness or other cause, to make their way out of the
shells. The beak is protruding, but it does not
seem to progress in its way round the shell. In
such instances the chick may be assisted by
gently chipping the shell away, or cracking it a
little distance from the beak each way. If the
membrane, which lies directly under the shell,
looks quite white and dry it may be torn a little
also, but on no account should it otherwise be
touched. To tear it before the embryo is ready
to hatch will cause profuse bleeding and death.
Generally speaking, however, chickens which
have to be thus assisted are seldom of much use,
and rather than irritate the hen by too much
attention, and delay the removal of the remaining chickens from the nest, we would sacrifice
the one or two which have not the strength to
extricate themselves.

Fallacy of Moistening the Nest.—As a rule, most people come to the very natural conclusion that when a chicken dies in the shell, having partly hatched, it has done so through lack of moisture. It has consequently become the habit to apply water to the nest in some way or other. The eggs are sprinkled, or a cupful of warm water is poured round the edge of the earthy

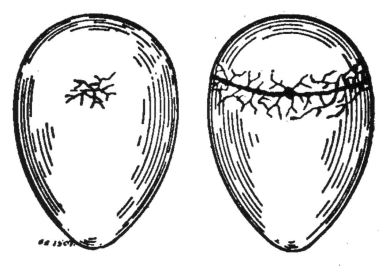

Fig. 10.—Eggs in Process of Hatching

foundation of the nest. That this is entirely a mistake has been proven beyond the shadow of a doubt. The nest may be as dry as tinder all through, and the eggs, other things being in order, will hatch perfectly well. There is not one egg in a thousand set naturally that fails to hatch through lack of moisture. If we go to Nature and see what her methods are in regard to this matter, what do we find? Nests placed in the driest situations. There are various devices for protecting the eggs against wet. On the Wood Pigeon's platform of sticks the eggs are exposed to the air, which is diffused through the coarsely-woven material on which they are laid. The Pheasant chooses the driest place available in which to lay her eggs. Wild Ducks leave the rivers for high ground, and sometimes nest on a ledge of rock, or even in the fork of a tree. Sheldrakes, another waterfowl, seek the dry, sandy rabbit-burrow in which to make their nests. And so one might go on citing instances to prove that moisture applied to the nest is a mistake. For many years we have set hens in the driest of nests in the driest of sheds, and even when the springs have been exceptionally rainless, with east wind blowing for weeks, the chickens—and ducklings, too—have invariably hatched well. Indeed, it is probable that more chickens are drowned in the shell than the contrary. An egg has sufficient moisture in itself to enable the chicken to extricate itself easily, and it is only when the eggs are exposed to excessive evaporation, as they are sometimes under artificial conditions, that moisture is necessary. For instance, in an hydro-incubator we apply water by means of a moisture tray. Why? Because the evaporation would otherwise be so great that the contents of the eggs would be dried up. The moisture and ventilation are made to balance each other, so that the egg neither loses its contents by undue evaporation nor the reverse. Let me persuade the beginner, therefore, to leave the water alone when dealing with sitting hens. If he has chickens " dead in the shell " let him look for other causes for the mortality.

CHAPTER VI

ARTIFICIAL INCUBATION

THE practice of hatching eggs artificially is older than history. The mammals, or egg-ovens, which may to-day be seen in Burma, and a few other places at the mouth of the Nile, extended at one period throughout the most important towns of the East. In these great incubators, crude as they are—being merely erections of "brick" heated by fires of straw and camel dung placed around the outer walls—the Egyptians hatch chickens with signal success. With no thermometers, thermostats, moisture trays, nor any of the other contrivances connected with a modern incubator, these primitive operators, with centuries of inherited practice at their backs, know not what failure is. From father to son the "secrets" of the profession have been handed down, and every year these huge "ovens"—sometimes measuring one hundred feet in length—turn out hundreds of thousands of chickens, and that against many of the most important principles of artificial incubation! Interesting as the subject is, space will not permit us to enter further into the matter, nor to give more than a brief glance at the history of incubation in later European times.

Earliest Type of Incubator.—The first serious attempts toward solving the problem of hatching chickens artificially were made in France, but most of them were attended with ill-success. Réaumur, apparently acting on the suggestion supplied by the mound-building turkey, already mentioned, hatched chickens fairly successfully under heaps of fermenting manure; but it was not until 1845 that the first incubator with a self-acting valve was constructed. It was invented by M. Vallée, of the Jardin des Plantes (Paris), and had a "run" of some notoriety. Then followed a series of others in this and other countries, which were all more or less impracticable owing to the constant watchfulness which they demanded on account of the imperfection of the regulating apparatus. England lent her talent to the subject and introduced several models, some of which did good work. But not only was it apparent that a reliable device for regulating temperature had yet to be discovered, but the relation between ventilation and moisture was a stumbling-block over which most of these early operators and inventors tripped.

First Type of Hydro-Incubators.—In 1877

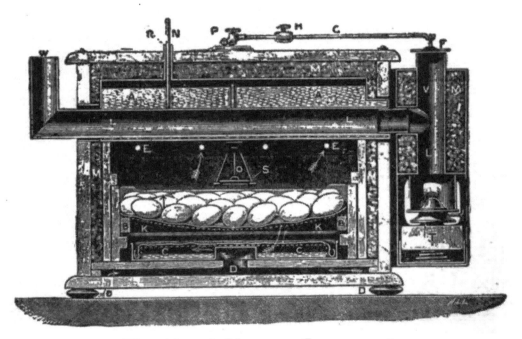

Fig. 11.—A MODERN INCUBATOR

the hydro-incubator was brought out, and it marked a step still further in the desired direction. But it was not until some years later, when a Mr. Hearson invented and patented his capsule regulator, that modern incubation was firmly established. With this little capsule the problem of automatic adjustment of temperature was mastered, and since the expiration of its patent most machines are fitted with it, or something similar to it. The student of incubation will here do well to understand what this capsule is made of, and how it works. We all know that when water boils the steam that is given off is hundreds of times greater in volume than the water; that if the lid of a kettle, even if only partly filled with water, were sealed down, the latter would burst owing to the expansion of the liquid within. Most liquids boil at certain temperatures under normal conditions—viz., water, 212 deg. F.; alcohol, 173 deg. F.; ether, 94 deg. F.; and all of these expand when they have attained their boiling-point. With that knowledge in mind, the inventors of the capsule introduced between two plates of brass a liquid which has been well called "compensated ether." The edges of the brass plates are soldered together, with the liquid in between. The obvious result is that when the capsule is subjected to heat it expands, owing to the vaporization of the liquid it contains, and the particular liquid which is used in making these capsules responds to a temperature of about 98 deg.

Features of a Modern Hydro-Incubator.—But before going on to discuss the actual working of the capsule and automatic regulation of the temperature which it to so great an extent ensures, it will be necessary to understand the other main features of a modern incubator. Almost all incubators are put together on the same principle, although they may differ in detail. At the upper part of the incubator in Fig. 11, a copper tank of water, AA, is placed, and through it a flue from the lamp is passed. In the illustration the flue, LL, is shown coming out on the left side of the machine, but in reality it traverses the length of the tank and returns, in horseshoe shape, to the end at which the lamp is situated. V is a chimney directly over the lamp, and upon it a damper, F, is resting, so that the whole of the heat must pass through the tank by way of the flue, LL. Raise the damper, however, and most, if not all, of the heat will escape at F, scarcely any passing through the tank. So it will be seen that by raising or lowering the damper we can increase or decrease the temperature of the tank, and, of course, the egg-chamber beneath it.

Now it is this regulation of temperature which is effected by the thermostatic capsule. In the

illustration the damper, F, is seen to be suspended
from a lever, G, which at its extreme left is
hinged to a metal casting. At a little distance
from the hinged end a piece of stiff wire, O,
passes downward, through a tube in the tank,
into the egg-chamber, its lowest extremity resting
on the thermostatic capsule, S, which is fixed to
a rigid metal bracket.

It will now be understood that we have, by
means of this wire or "connecting-rod," a direct
communication between the egg-chamber and the
lever and damper. Moreover, we shall see how
this regulating apparatus becomes automatic.
Supposing that the incubator is working at the
required temperature, the damper being about
one eighth of an inch off the top of the chimney,
and we take the egg-drawer out for a few minutes, we find the damper almost immediately
sinks upon the chimney, owing to the flattening
of the capsule on account of the lowering of the
temperature. But replace the drawer, allow the
heat to accumulate, and the capsule will again be
distended. The wire, O, resting upon it, will be
pushed upward, with the result that the lever is
raised and the damper again lifted off the
chimney.

It will be understood, therefore, that when once this apparatus is properly regulated, it scarcely matters how high or how low (within reasonable limits) the lamp flame may be, the temperature will be kept uniform. Any excess of heat will make the capsule bulge, raise the damper, and so let it pass out of the chimney rather than through the tank. And, on the contrary, if the outside temperature is low or the lamp flame insufficient, the little damper will lie flat on the chimney, sending all the available heat into the tank. On this principle all modern regulating devices are constructed. Thermostats differ very considerably, as we shall see, but the lever and damper are common to all.

Turning again to the illustration, we see the walls of the incubator are packed with some non-conductive material, MM. The egg-tray, KK, has a bottom of perforated zinc, which is slightly concave, so that the outer eggs, which are naturally cooler than those in the centre, will be nearer the source of heat than the latter. DD are holes to admit air, and this traverses a water tray, over which is placed a damp piece of sacking, passes upward between the eggs, and escapes at the holes, EE, at the back of the machine.

Non-Moisture Incubators.—A comparatively few years ago a "non-moisture" incubator was brought out in the United States. For some time operators were sceptical of these machines, which had no tank and no applied moisture.

Fig. 12.—CYPHER'S NON-MOISTURE INCUBATOR

Now, however, they are as generally used as the others, and there is no doubt that they have won their reputation upon merit. Fig. 12 represents one of these machines, of which it is not difficult to understand the working. At one end there is a lamp, the heat from which passes up the

middle and down the outside of a "heater."
Through a separate chamber in this latter the
fresh air, being first warmed, owing to its coming in contact with the walls of the flue, enters
directly into the top of the machine. It then
passes downward through a porous diaphragm
of felt-like substance into the egg-chamber.
Continuing through the egg-drawer of wire
gauze, it again percolates through a double
diaphragm, and escapes at the bottom. There
are no ventilating holes whatever (excepting one
underneath, which is seldom opened), for it will
be seen that the constant flow of fresh, warm air
through the machine is sufficient. But it is in
the slowness of this circulation that the secret
lies. The air is diffused as it traverses the incubator, and the ventilation, which is also the
source of heat, is a purely "molecular" one.
We must, however, return to this part of the
subject later.

The Thermostat used in these incubators consists of two or more strong strips of steel with
alternate strips of aluminium or zinc in between,
all being riveted together at each end. A connecting-rod passing through the base of the

lever, where it balances on a knife-edge, downward through the incubator is buttoned top and bottom by a nut working on a thread. Now, when the thermostat is subjected to heat, the

Fig. 13.—REMOVING THE DIAPHRAGMS

aluminium (or zinc) expands, and as the latter is fixed to the steel at either end there is nothing for it but to bow, or bulge. The result is that the connecting-rod tightens on the base of the lever, causing the damper to lift off the chimney, and the apparatus, once it is adjusted, is perfectly self-regulating to half a degree. The principle is the same as that before described, the difference being only in the thermostat.

Improvements in Incubators.—Many improvements have been made in later times upon these atmospheric incubators, chief of which may be mentioned the adoption of removable diaphragms for cleaning purposes. All air is laden with fine particles of dust, and the pores of the felt must in time become choked, rendering free circulation impossible. Now the operator can remove all diaphragms, give them a good brushing and airing, and replace them in a few minutes. Another " improvement," from the buyer's point of view, is the price of these incubators, as well as others. Competition has rendered it necessary for all manufacturers to reduce the retail cost of their machines down to reasonable figures.

Having briefly described the general working principles of the usual types of incubators, the beginner will be to some extent prepared for practical operations. Many important details have been omitted, but these will be referred to as occasion arises in the next few pages.

CHAPTER VII

ARTIFICIAL INCUBATION IN PRACTICE

SOME consideration must be given to the room in which the incubator is to work. Some years ago many people supposed that a cellar, often damp and musty, was the most suitable place to run the machine in, the idea, no doubt, having arisen in that erroneous belief regarding the necessity for moisture already referred to. On the other hand, a cellar is usually quiet and its temperature even, and on that account, always supposing it to be fairly dry and well ventilated (this is essential), it may make a suitable operating room. Any ordinary room, however, will do, provided it is of a fairly normal temperature, has efficient ventilation without draught, is in a quiet place, and so built that it is free from vibration. A vacant bedroom often serves as an excellent operating place if the floor is tolerably firm.

Placing the Incubator.—Always place the incubator so that the lamp is not in a direct draught, such as may exist between the door and the chimney. Tank machines, not being sold with legs, must be placed on a table or their own packing case, and these incubators especially must be set quite level. Those which have glass doors to the egg-chambers ought to face the light, so that the thermometer may be read without difficulty.

Temperature.—Full directions being always sent out with each incubator, it would serve no useful purpose here to enter into the subject of putting the machine together and setting it going. Any intelligent beginner can, by studying the simple directions, get along all right, so far as the actual working is concerned. Moreover, all machines differ in minute points, and their respective makers should know how to instruct the beginner if any one does. It must, however, be borne in mind that incubators, even though they be "automatic self-regulating," are only so within certain limits. Frequent regulation may be necessary when the outside temperature is very variable. Most operators, for instance, find it gives better results if, say, the machine is running at 104 deg., with an outside temperature (*i. e.*, in the room) of 60 deg., they increase the heat of the egg-chamber 1 deg. for every 10 deg. decrease below the 60 deg., and vice versa. Thus the thermometer on or near the eggs should stand at 105 deg. when the room is at 50 deg., or at 103 deg. with an outside temperature of 70 deg. Generally speaking, when the chickens hatch late—after the twenty-first day—it indicates a lack of heat during the process of incubation. On the other hand, if the eggs begin to chip early, say on the eighteenth or nineteenth day, one may generally put it down to an excessive temperature. This connection between the heat of the room and that of the incubators placed in it is a very important one, and should not be lost sight of at any time. It is not desirable to run an incubator in winter in a room that seldom rises above 45 deg. at that season.

An even temperature is, of course, very essential to successful hatching. Most incubator manufacturers recommend a temperature of 104 deg. in the centre of the egg tray when the room is about normal. In atmospherics we have found that 102½ deg. to 103 deg., as recommended by some of their American makers, is too low unless the room is very warm indeed, and that 104 deg., with a hatching temperature of 105 deg., is better.

Placing the Eggs in the Incubator.—Before the eggs are placed in the incubator (see Chap. IV) the latter should have been going steadily for a couple of days. It naturally follows that when a tray of cold eggs is put into a warm chamber the temperature of the latter quickly runs down, and it is some hours before it regains its proper level. Morning is therefore the best time to start actual operations, for then one can see the temperature readjusted before nightfall.

Management of an Incubator.—The directions supplied with the machine must not only be intelligently carried out in respect to the regulating, etc., of the machine, but also as regards the care of the lamp. The best oil must be used, and a new wick each time the incubator is reset should replace the old one. Every day at a certain hour the lamp must be " trimmed," and that implies thorough cleaning. When once the wick burns straight, without tails, it should never be cut, but have the crust wiped off with a bit of flannel, and the surface smoothed down with some flat object, such as the blade of a knife.

There must be a good flame burning always, and with a little practice it will not be difficult to get it the same height every day. If the flame is too high or too low, smoking occurs, which chokes the flues, so obstructing the free circulation of heat. Where gas can be obtained we would have it fitted to all machines which are adapted for it. Even where there is no local gas supply it would pay extensive operators to utilize acetylene or gasoline. Lamps are, at the best, messy things, and the work they entail is considerable when a number of incubators are at work.

Turning the Eggs.—During the first twenty-four hours the eggs are best left alone; after that, and until the eighteenth day (we are speaking of hens' eggs) they must be turned twice daily. On each occasion they should be given a half-turn only, and the first thing in the morning and last thing before dark are the best occasions for the operation. It is advantageous also to occasionally change the relative positions of the eggs in the drawer, those from the centre being placed at the side, and the reverse. In the non-moisture incubators referred to already the inclined trays and method of moving and turning a whole row of eggs with one movement obviate the necessity for so much handling. As soon as the eggs are turned, on the first occasion in the mornings, the trays may at once be replaced in the incubator, but in the evening the eggs must be left out for an "airing." The period allotted for this must depend upon the season or temperature, and also upon the age of the embryos. For the first week less airing is required than in later days. If it is very cold, five minutes during the first eight days and then ten will be enough, but in warm weather eggs may often be left out for more than twice as long. Indeed, it is probable that embryos more often suffer from insufficient airing than the contrary. The eggs should never be placed in a direct draught when out of the incubator, and they must on all occasions be handled gently.

Object of Turning the Eggs.—In turning and airing the eggs we are doing no more than the sitting hen does. She daily, by a shuffling movement of her body, not only turns the eggs but moves their positions in the nest. And if we refer to Chapter II we can understand how necessary this turning is. The yolk of the egg we read, floats in the albumen, and carries on its upper surface the germ-spot, from which life

Fig. 14.—A Special Incubator House

begins. As it is lighter than the albumen, and the chalazæ are attached rather below the line of its axis, or diameter, it rides high, being separated from the shell by a comparatively thin layer of albumen only. Now if the egg is always left on one side, that thin layer of albumen is apt to evaporate, which means that the yolk adheres to the shell, and the germ dies. But if we turn the eggs round, a fresh quantity of albumen is every time brought between the yolk and the shell, so that such an accident as the yolk sticking and the egg becoming addled is prevented.

Testing the Eggs.—Some time between the seventh and ninth days the eggs should be tested, the object being to remove the unfertile ones. The operation is a simple one, and with a little practice one can carry it out without the assistance of any elaborate apparatus. Too much testing, as we have already said, is not desirable, and in the case of artificial incubation the beginner must be very careful that he does not get the eggs chilled during the process. He is particularly liable to do this when there is a large tray of eggs to get through, and it must be remembered that the embryo is more delicate, more susceptible to extremes of temperature, when at about a week old than at any other time. A piece of warm flannel spread over the egg tray while testing is going on will often prevent chilling.

Chilled Eggs.—Accidents not infrequently happen during incubation. The hen may suddenly forsake her nest, leaving the eggs to become cold; the incubator lamp may go out; or the operator may forget to replace the trays in the machines after airing, with the same result. During the first week or ten days of incubation eggs that have been quite chilled seldom recover, but at any time after that the embryos, if they are strong, can stand great extremes. If only a few eggs, say a hen's clutch, have become chilled, the best thing to do with them is to immerse them in a pail of water that is just comfortably warm to the hand. There they may be left until another hen is procured; or they may remain there for five or ten minutes and then be put in an incubator that is already going. It is a more difficult matter when a whole tray of eggs have been chilled, and the best one can do is to dip a square of flannel in water heated to about 105 deg., wring it, lay it over the eggs, and place the tray in the incubator—the door of the latter being open just enough to allow the steam to escape. Such measures, if promptly carried out, will often save a hatch.

Fig. 15.—A Good Hatch—Forty-nine Chickens
from Fifty Eggs

Overheated Eggs.—Eggs subjected to a temperature that is too high are not so easily revived, although it is difficult to say what the "baking-point" is. During the first ten days exposure to 110 deg. or 112 deg. for a few hours will often kill every embryo, whereas later on it appears to have but little effect. There is not much that can be done for such eggs beyond instantly removing them, and airing until a thermometer with its bulb resting on an egg (not an unfertile one) stands at about 60 deg.

Thermometers and Their Use.—A word or two here, before going on, with regard to thermometers will not be out of place. Everything depends upon these instruments, and they must consequently be absolutely reliable. Cheap ones are an abomination. Most of those sent out by incubator makers are tested and well-seasoned, but if there is any doubt as to their correctness the operator may test them for himself. The doubtful one may be tested by comparison with one that is known to be reliable, both being subjected to the same heat. If a thermometer be inverted and gently tapped, the mercury should run down to the bottom, thus showing the complete exclusion of air in the tube. Immersed in ice the thermometer should stand at 32 deg. If held in the steam issuing from the spout of a boiling kettle (care being taken not to immerse it too suddenly, or it may break), the mercury ought to register 212 deg. Scarcely five per cent. of the cheap instruments seen in shop windows can stand these simple trials.

Moisture and Ventilation.—Equally important as the proper temperature is the right proportion between moisture and ventilation. The two are inseparably connected, but it has taken makers of incubators down to the most recent times to thoroughly grasp that fact, and make their machines accordingly. In the earlier attempts at incubation the chickens either died in the shell through insufficient ventilation, or they were "dried up" through having too much. Then people went to the other extremes, and, hoping to balance matters, moisture was used too lavishly, with the result that the embryos were "drowned," the moisture being in excess of the evaporation. It was a long time before manufacturers of hydro-incubators mastered this subject. Even to-day some of them are apt to stumble over it.

The beginner who wishes to become a successful operator must see clearly through this subject of ventilation and moisture. If he begins
with the knowledge that an egg has sufficient
moisture in itself for all its needs, and that it will
hatch successfully without any being added to it,
so long as it is not robbed of that moisture which
it has, he will be half-way toward understanding
the question. We have referred to this subject
at the end of Chapter V, and a study of eggs
being incubated under natural conditions is of
the utmost value.

It has been said that we may look at a hen
sitting for a lifetime and not gather much infor-
mation. Reading literally, we may take it that
the writer was speaking for himself! One of the
many lessons that we can learn of the sitting
hen, or wild bird, is that she not only for choice
selects a quiet, dry place for her nest, but that
the eggs she sits upon are entirely covered by her
feathers. Yet this covering is exceedingly light.
It is essentially porous, allowing the air to have
free access to the eggs from all sides. There is,
however, no rapid circulation of air, no draughts,
no evaporating currents. The circulation is
" molecular." The air is slowly diffused through

the screen of feathers. This fact the later makers of incubators began to realize and work upon. Again, do not the old egg-ovens of Egypt hatch eggs with unfailing success? And in them there is practically no draught and no moisture.

It was these facts which not only led to the adoption of "non-moisture" incubators, but to the better balancing of ventilation and moisture in the hydros. If we refer again to the diagram of the incubator (Fig. 11), we shall see that the air enters at the bottom of the machine, passes through a piece of sacking which is kept wet, traverses the egg-chamber, and escapes at EE. Now if it were not for the moisture taken up by the air the eggs, owing to the rapid evaporation caused by direct currents of air, would become "dried up." The fresh air is, however, essential, as we have seen. It cannot be shut out, so we counteract its evaporating effect by making it take up moisture when it enters the egg-chamber. And the makers of this type of machine have now got the due proportion between moisture and ventilation just about perfect. Of course we know that the quantity of aqueous vapor which the air takes up depends on the temperature, but then, so long as we can maintain an even temperature in the egg-chamber, the amount of moisture will not vary.

It will now be understood how important it is to keep the moisture trays properly filled when working an incubator. The piece of sacking as well as the tray on which it rests should be well scalded with hot water and a little carbolic after every hatch, otherwise the air entering the machine is liable to be fouled.

The reader will now, perhaps, be able to see also why atmospheric incubators, like those mentioned in Chapter VI, do not require added moisture. The principle of the circulation of the air through porous diaphragms is the same as Nature has adopted in the case of the sitting hen. It is because there is no undue evaporation by direct currents of air that moisture is not required. And the doubt that was cast upon the efficacy of this class of machine when first introduced is being entirely dispelled by the success which attends the use of them. Was it not ever the same with things that are new, that depart so far from the accustomed type?

Failures and Their Causes.—If the beginner has a run of failures which he cannot account for, a

study of the air-cell (see Fig. 2) will often help
him to elucidate the mystery. At the commence-
ment of incubation, or in a fresh egg, the air-cell
will be very small, but as development progresses
we find it steadily increasing through evaporation. It has been found that while, as we have
already seen, too much evaporation is injurious to
the developing embryo, a certain amount for the
proper enlargement of the air-cell is just as essential. An excess of moisture during incubation
means that the contents of the egg are reduced
so little by evaporation that the chicken at the
point of hatching is too big for the egg. It so
fills the space that it cannot turn round, which it
must do to extricate itself. On the contrary, if
the evaporation has been too great, and the
moisture insufficient, the chicken will be too small.
It will be tied down, as it were, by a tough
and leathery membrane, and not infrequently
"glued" to the shell.

No hard and fast rules can be laid down with
regard to the treatment of eggs from a study of
their air-cells, and too much fussing and med-
dling is as bad as no attention at all. But by a
careful study of the air-cells when testing, and at
hatching time, by keeping a record of the tem-

perature, weather, and other details, and by an intelligent comparison of results, the operator will ultimately be able to tell fairly accurately whether his eggs are going on all right, and if they are not he will not be without a remedy.

After the Eighteenth Day.—The eggs in the incubator tray should not be turned after the eighteenth or nineteenth day, but a moderate airing until the first one begins to chip (Fig. 10) is desirable. After that the drawer should not be opened oftener than is absolutely necessary. And here we would urge again for the more universal use of glass doors or backs to incubators, so that the operator can see what is going on inside without opening the egg-chamber. Great as that advantage is, it is only one of the many that might be mentioned in favor of glass doors.

At hatching time, and a little before, the temperature will naturally increase in the incubator, and it may be allowed to do so to some extent. In very cold weather we have found 105 deg. to 106 deg. not too high for atmospheric incubators, and rather less for the others. With a room at 40 deg. to 45 deg. during the day, and less than that at night (not that we would recommend such a place to others), we have hatched most successfully at a regular temperature of 108 deg. during the last two days! That was going to extremes, but it serves to show that the beginner must watch other things than the thermometer in the incubator.

Newly-hatched Chicks.—When a good number of chickens are hatched they should be removed to the "drying-box," and at the same time the empty shells may be cleared out. This must be done quickly, however, and the drawer immediately closed. In most atmospheric incubators, there is a far better way of disposing of the chickens as they hatch. The egg-tray is somewhat narrower than the back-to-front measurement of the chamber, so that there is a space between it and the glass front of two or three inches. When the chickens hatch they crawl toward the glass and topple over into the "nursery" below. This latter is "floored" by one of the diaphragms already mentioned, and it is, of course, several degrees cooler than in the tray above it. Here the chickens can be fed and left for a few days, if necessary, in a condition which is impossible, if only on account of size, in ordinary "drying-boxes." Of course, as they are now made, this plan could not be adopted by hydro-incubators.

General Remarks.—The same remarks, as regards the treatment of eggs during hatching, and especially of those which appear to require help, which we have made on page 44, apply equally here, and with those, together with the directions sent out with all good incubators, the intelligent novice should be able to get along fairly well. Having chickens " dead in the shell " will be his most frequent cry, and some of the causes for this we have already pointed out in Chapter V.

Let it be ever remembered that, although there are some death-traps called incubators on the market, failure is far more often due to the eggs themselves or the operator than to the machine. And, finally, let it be borne in mind that when we have an indifferent hatch from an incubator, the failure and disappointment appear so much greater because of the number of eggs concerned. We are generally satisfied if we get eight strong chickens out of a dozen eggs incubated by a hen, but if we had twelve dozen eggs in an incubator

and hatched ninety-six chickens, leaving nearly
sixty eggs to account for, would we be so satisfied ? Some of us would write an irate letter to
the maker of the machine, and do and say various
unreasonable things which a little thought might
prevent, because the percentage of failures is the
same in both instances, only in the one it is
brought into higher relief.

CHAPTER VIII

REARING THE CHICKENS WITH HENS

HAVING hatched a brood of chickens, the first thing to do is to remove them and the hen to a suitable coop. This must be amply large enough (not less than eighteen inches each way) and waterproof, but it need not be an expensive affair.

A good coop may be made out of a sugar-box by any amateur joiner, and such a one will last for many years with an occasional application of tar or paint. If it be for use in the open, and the great majority of coops are, it must be storm-proof. Furthermore, it is always desirable to nail two stout ribs of wood across the bottom, one on each side, so as to keep it off the damp ground. The front must be made of two or three movable bars of wood fixed in a perpendicular position, and a night shutter is essential, more for the purpose of keeping out vermin than for protection against cold. Indeed, it will be found that overheating and stuffiness are the main evils to be avoided in chicken-rearing, and that fresh air, even if it be cold, so long as it is not in the nature of a draught, is an element which the rearer cannot afford to ignore.

Floors to Coops.—There is much difference of opinion upon the desirability of having floors to coops, but most practical rearers admit that in the early months of the year they are a great help to the chickens. There is another argument, and a very strong one, in favor of floors, and that is they economize not only the ground in the rearing place, but the manure is saved. A coop that has not a floor must be frequently moved on to fresh turf, and the inevitable result is, especially where a number are in use, that a very large area of ground soon becomes very effectually fouled. Where rearing is done late in the season, and space is of little consideration —as in the case of pheasant-rearing—then bottomless coops may be employed with advantage.

Position for the Coops.—While preparing the coop for the reception of the brood, the hen may be given a good meal of grain, or barley-meal and middlings, while she is still on the nest, the food being placed in a small tin or feeder. At the same time it will be well to notice that the chickens are all right, and that they cannot tumble out of the nest or into corners and so get lost or chilled. Put the coop in a sunny situation on dry, short turf, if possible, or a garden path. Where rearing is done somewhat extensively a piece of ground should already have been prepared as a nursery, and in it the coops or brooders may be placed in rows at a convenient distance apart. The coop must be littered with dry earth or peat-moss. If the weather is very cold some chaff may be sprinkled over the former. Some hens, when placed in the coop first, commence scratching and shuffling so vigorously in the litter that the chickens often get hurt or half-buried, if not killed. To avoid this, it is a good plan to get an old sack, fold it into a square the size of the coop bottom, and lay it on the litter. It can remain there until the chickens are a little stronger, say for a couple of days, and then be removed. If the coops are all of about the same size a few squares of old heavy carpet may be kept entirely for this purpose.

Placing the Chicks in the Coop.—The chickens should be carried from the nest to the coop in a small canvas-lined basket, such as those used for carrying bantams or pigeons to and from shows, when there will be no fear of their being chilled by sudden exposure to cold winds. This precaution is even more important when removing chickens from the incubator to the brooder. The hen being put into the coop, and the young ones after her, the next move should be to provide the latter with their first meal.

The Chicks' First Meal.—For the first meal there is nothing like the old-fashioned hard-boiled egg and stale bread crumbs, the former being well minced and mixed up with the latter. A little of this should be sprinkled upon the sack, and the chickens will in most cases immediately begin to eat. In a couple of hours or so another meal may be given, and the following day some coarse oatmeal may be added to the mixture. Unfertile eggs are just as good as fresh ones for the chickens, but this food should not be used exclusively nor excessively, and not after the third day, unless the chickens are very weak and the weather against them. Having discontinued it gradually, some scalded biscuit-meal may be given with the oatmeal, and green food added to the bill of fare. One could not well exaggerate the importance of a good supply of fresh, juicy vegetables, particularly while there is no spring growth on the turf. Lettuce, cabbage, and onions can always be obtained and the last-named is an excellent vegetable for chickens if minced up. They are cheap, always obtainable, wholesome, and prevent many diseases.

Feeding the Chicks Later On.—When the chickens have taken to the oatmeal and biscuit-meal some dry food may be introduced, a little at each meal until the birds get accustomed to it. Or some can be put in a small trough so that the chickens can help themselves. But before going on it would be as well here to say something more as regards " dry-feed." Briefly, it is a collection of seeds or broken grain mixed together in varying proportions, and when it was brought out, only a year or two ago, it was recommended to rear chickens " from the shell " upon it. It was a new thing, and people went to extremes with it, and fed chickens with " dry-feed " from hatching time onward. And no doubt they succeeded, but not so well as if they had used some soft food also, most particularly in the earlier stages. Now "dry-feed" has settled down into its proper place in the chickens' menu. With most practical feeders it is made the staple diet, especially for those birds which are destined for stock, and in which a steady growth is desirable. Its main virtues are these: It is easy to use; there is no mixing to be done, and no likelihood of it ever becoming sour if not all eaten up by the chickens. It stimulates the gizzard and other digestive organs of the birds, thus promoting health, and to a great extent prevents diarrhœa. It may be used to sprinkle in litter to encourage scratching exercise, which is impossible with soft foods; it undoubtedly promotes feather growth, and is more sustaining when given as a last feed in the evening. For rapid development, however, such as is desired in market stock, there is no doubt that a larger proportion of soft food (which is more quickly assimilated) is better, giving grain, say, about twice daily—letting one of these feeds be the last at night. Of course, in one sense "dry-feed" is only an old thing under a new name. Broken wheat, millet, and other grains were used long ago but it is only quite recently that those who cater for the chickens have offered the mixture of seeds and kibbled grain known as "dry-feed" to the poultry-keeping public.

Exercise for the Chicks.—As soon as the chickens are strong enough to move about they should be allowed access to a small run placed in front of the coop. The advantages derived from using such a run are manifold. In the early spring the wooden sides protect the chickens from the cold winds. The brood is kept together, and the individuals learn to know their own coop. If there be no such restriction of liberty some of the youngsters are often liable to wander round to the back of the coop, where they may succumb to exposure or be picked up by vermin. Feeding must be done outside the coop, in the run, as soon as possible, and every encouragement given to get the chickens out. The hen must not be forgotten, and it is as well to give her a good feed of grain and some water twice daily. When there is only one or two broods being reared, and the weather is fine, it is often wise to let the mothers roam with their chickens, but that is impossible when there are many coops occupied. Care must, however,

be taken to notice that the hens do not over-
tire the chickens, nor trail them through wet
grass.

Feeding after the Tenth Day.—When ten days
or a fortnight old the chickens may have a
further change of diet. Instead of using oatmeal, which is expensive, some fine middlings
may be mixed with the biscuit-meal ; and it will
be as well to say here that when scalding the
latter, or, indeed, mixing water with anything
for young chickens, one should not use any more
liquid than is absolutely necessary. An excess
of fluid in meals—such as biscuit-meal especially
—will assuredly be followed by diarrhœa. Rice,
if it can be had at not over four or five cents
per pound, is a good and economical food to be
used incidentally with others. It must, however,
be boiled, well rinsed through with cold water,
and strained before it is fit to use, and in that
condition it will keep fresh several days. Just
before feeding add to it a little fine middlings,
and stir into a crumbly state. Being of an as-
tringent nature, rice is valuable as a preventive
of diarrhœa, but it must not be fed in a sloppy
or sticky condition. There is much difference of

opinion upon the question of giving animal meat to young chickens, but most rearers agree that they are better without it until about a fortnight old. Then, in limited quantities, there is no doubt that it assists development, and helps to build up strong constitutions. The kind of meat which we have found to be the safest is that known as " dried " or " granulated." It must be scalded before use, and it is best to give it as an extra meal by itself, about once a day, or oftener as the chickens grow up. It is not an easy matter to say how much meat may be given, because so much depends upon the time of year, age and size of the chickens, and other circumstances. But under normal conditions a dozen chickens of a fortnight old may have a good tablespoonful measured before scalding at noon each day. Green bone should not be given until the birds are well feathered—say eight to ten weeks old—but bone meal, or " bone dust," as it is sometimes called, is useful right through the rearing process. For birds that are destined for stock, in particular, it may be strongly recommended. It assists the formation of bone, goes far toward preventing crooked breasts (turkey rearers may take that hint), and in the earlier

stages of growth it acts as a preventive of diarrhœa.

Feeding after the Third Week.—At the age of
three weeks to a month the feeding, while being
sufficiently good, may be conducted on still
cheaper lines. Biscuit-meal may be gradually
dispensed with, or only given once a day, and instead of it ground oats be used. This latter, if

Fig. 16.—A Flower-Pot Water Vessel for Chicks

mixed with an equal proportion of middlings,
makes an excellent food, and it is one that can
be kept in stock from this stage right through to
maturity. Then there is maize meal, which, if
scalded with boiling water and stirred crumbly
when cold, or nearly so, with middlings, will
make a useful change at any time for the
broods. "Dry-feed," as before described, may
also be gradually stopped, and wheat given in-

stead, and the latter can be often substituted by corn (cracked or " kibbled "), barley, and buckwheat.

Many people have facilities for obtaining what might be called here " local products "—such as stale bread, brewer's grains, potato, and scraps from hotels, and these all come in useful if fed judiciously. Bread ought to have some fat with it, or, soaked in milk, it will make a food that chickens will thrive on. Scraps from the table must be sweet and clean, and if well boiled and mixed crumbly with middlings, after being minced or chopped, they will afford a useful change of diet. Potato is too starchy for general use (peelings should not be fed at all), but mashed with middlings and a little milk is very valuable for the bigger chickens as they approach the market stage. Milk itself deserves special mention, for whenever it can be obtained fairly cheap it ought to be used. Meals such as those mentioned above may be mixed with it, or it can be given to the chickens as a drink once or twice daily. The great value of milk for fattening purposes has long been recognized in those districts of England where that branch of the industry is made a speciality.

Water for Chickens.—A few years ago there was an almost universal outcry among rearers against allowing the chickens water. It was said to foster disease—gapes and diarrhœa in particular—and to be no end of trouble. If chickens had never tasted it they would never want it. There was sufficient water in the soft food, and any addition to that was excessive. These and other arguments were brought forward, and chickens were, there is no doubt, reared very successfully on the "total abstinence" system. But whether the mortality was any less is another question. However, that was before the era of dry-feeding came in. With this water became a necessity on account of the nature of the food, and to-day it is, or ought to be, in general use. Even in the days before dry-feeding was adopted it was not wise to try to rear chickens without water, for when judiciously used it has always proved a preservative of health rather than the reverse. Gapes, diarrhœa, excessive drinking, and other evils only occur when the supply is either impure or irregular. A constant allowance of water that is pure and kept out of the sun, in vessels that are clean, is an invigorating tonic. It is one of

Nature's greatest gifts, and is just as essential to life as the air we breathe. But, on the other hand, and like the air, it must be pure, or it im-

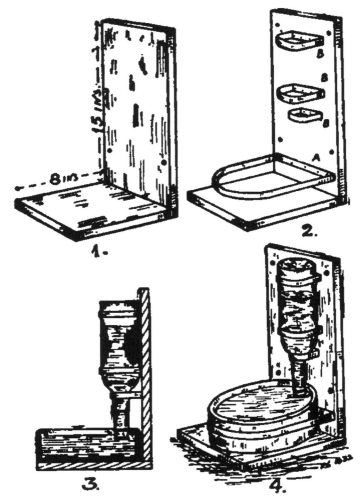

Fig. 17.—Bottle Fountain for Supplying Water for Chicks

mediately becomes a source of disease. There is one other argument in favor of giving water, and it is this. It often happens that we have to give tonics or medicines to chickens, and the water is the most convenient medium through which to do it.

Grit for Chickens.—Next to water, grit ranks high in importance, especially now that there is so much grain used. It is essential to the general health of the birds, and a small box of it should always be within reach. Just as in the case of water, the supply must be good and regular or trouble will follow. The best grits to use are those sold properly prepared for chickens, and they are cheap enough. Sand is of no use whatever, but fine gravel from the bed of a fresh-water stream will often serve the purpose. This latter is particularly good for ducklings. Grit should never be mixed with the food in any case.

Number of Meals per Day.—So far no mention has been made as to the number of meals which chickens should have each day, excepting that at the very first every two hours is not too frequent, provided a little only is given at a time. After that the feeder must rely upon his own judgment rather than the clock. He must feed the chickens when they are hungry, and give them as much as they will clear up, without leaving any for the wild birds and vermin.

Dry-feed, it is true, may often be placed in troughs or scattered in litter, but generally speaking the youngsters must be so fed that they get quite enough at each meal, and are ready with a good appetite for that meal when it comes. The happy medium between starvation or insufficiency on the one side, and excess or overindulgence on the other, must be struck before one can rear successfully. The chickens' appetites, which will vary with the season, the daily weather or temperature, the kind of food used, the age of the birds themselves, and many other things, must be the feeder's guidance. If he begins by too much rule-of-thumb, and not enough common sense and observation, he will never be a success. His must be a mind that is plastic, capable of taking in every little thing he sees about him, and acting accordingly.

If he has no reliance in himself, no practical experience to back him up ; if he must adjust his spectacles, study the table of weights and measures, worry his brain unnecessarily about "carbo-hydrates" or the exactitudes of "al-

buminoid ratios " and " digestion co-efficients "—
all estimable things in their way—he may as
well give up chicken rearing and become an
analytical chemist at once.

Weaning the Chickens.—At any time between
the ages of five to ten weeks, according to the
time of year and other circumstances, the chickens
may be considered weaned. They will be fairly
well feathered, and able to keep themselves warm
enough at night without the hen. Indeed, as a
general rule, the latter is kept too long with her
chickens, with the result that they get overheated
at night, and disease follows. The conditions
under which the rearing is being done must, of
course, always be studied. One would not, for
instance, take the mother away from her brood
just at the beginning of a sudden spell of cold
weather. And the rearer would be a duffer indeed who kept the brood and hen together in a
stuffy coop in hot summer weather just because
a book happened to give either eight or ten weeks
as the proper age for the separation.

If the coops are large, small broods may be
amalgamated for a week or ten days after leaving the hen. There will then be one of the coops

vacant for further use, and the chickens will not be so likely to take cold, a large lot naturally keeping warmer than a small one. But when once they are weaned their occupation of the original coops should not cover more than about a fortnight, that period being sufficiently long as an intermediary break, during which the young-sters may gain not only independence but hardi-hood.

After this, larger houses must be employed, even those used for adults not being too big, for it will be necessary to run the young stock in lots of forty or so. The individuals in these flocks should be as nearly as possible of the same age, and if heavy and light breeds be kept apart the latter will do better. The sexes must be sep-arated as soon as the cockerels begin to crow— or rather before that—the pens occupied by each being placed as far apart as possible.

It is well to bear in mind before going on, that to succeed with market stock or adults one must have the birds reared well. Everything depends on the first ten weeks or so. Weaknesses con-tracted then, through disease or indifferent atten-tion, will, in nearly every case, follow the bird through life. It is the chicken that has healthy, robust parents; the chicken that is hatched in good time, and hatched well; the chicken that is brought up in healthy surroundings, and by practiced hands, that pays, and becomes a credit to its owner.

CHAPTER IX

ARTIFICIAL REARING

ALTHOUGH there are many people who, for various reasons, still stick to " the old hen," the wide and ever-increasing popularity of incubators has rendered the production of foster-mothers absolutely necessary. Some few prefer to hatch artificially, transferring the chickens to hens at hatching time, but, generally speaking, where there is an incubator there must be a foster-mother in which to bring up the chickens.

Foster-Mothers.—The best of these appliances are now made in two types, just as the incubators are, viz., those heated by a tank of hot water, and others by hot air. While passing over the earlier patterns of foster-mothers—all of which are now practically obsolete—it will be as well here to briefly mention the characteristics of those which are now in daily use, so that the novice may gain some insight into the general arrangement of such appliances. At one end there is a tank of water, which is heated by a lamp (see illustrations), and this tank warms the sleeping compartment, or hottest part of the rearer. The heat of the lamp also serves to slightly raise the temperature of the larger chamber, which may be seen fronted with fine wire-netting and sheets of glass which are mov-

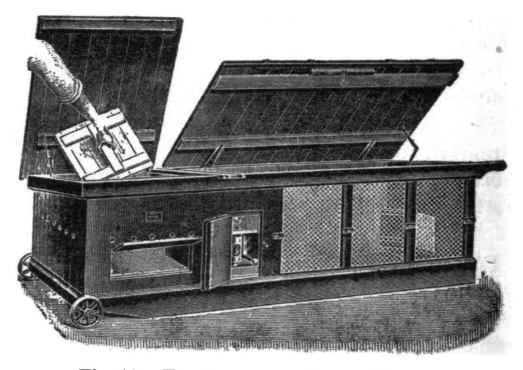

Fig. 18.—THE INCUBATOR FOSTER MOTHER

able or adjustable. Machines of this kind are absolutely storm-proof, and constructed for outdoor work.

In the atmospheric foster-mothers the lamp is placed underneath the sleeping place. This heats a galvanized-iron sheeting, which is directly under the floor of the dormitory. Over this sheeting a shaft of tin extends from the chickens' chamber to the outer air. This gets heated by the lamp below, so that a constant flow of fresh, warm air is passing into the dormitory and out at the ventilating holes above. No lamp fumes can possibly enter the brooder in any way.

FIG. 19.--ATMOSPHERIC FOSTER-MOTHER

In the atmospheric foster-mother the plan is rather different. The heat of the lamp is conducted up a metal pipe or chimney into the chickens' chamber above, where it enters a large round air tank or drum. Here it circulates twice over a radiator, and from thence passes out into a compartment above, which is in direct communication with the outer air. The fresh air enters from outside, and, in entering, it is thoroughly warmed by coming in contact with the lamp flue. The result is a constant flow of fresh, warm air into the dormitory, and an even distribution of heat from the air tank, which extends above the chickens' heads. In the illustration the sliding roof is drawn back and lids of inner compartment thrown open.

Selecting a Foster-Mother.—There are a number of good foster-mothers on the market, and, as we have already pointed out, those which are here described and illustrated are given for the purpose of representation rather than of comparison and criticism. In selecting a foster-mother the beginner must (eschewing all those savoring of cheapness) look to certain well-defined points in construction and plan. To begin with (we are speaking now of outdoor rearers), it must be well built, storm-proof, and substantial. A toy of a thing means disappointment, loss, and often serious fires. There must be plenty of room in it, and any amount of light. In this last respect manufacturers are somewhat shy. They scarcely give any window at all to the hot chamber, the very place where it is needed, for it is when they are in there (whether during the first day or so, or at night throughout the period of rearing) that the chickens require closest observation. To open the lid every time one wants to see how things are going on inside means escape of heat, if not a serious chilling of the inmates; it disturbs the chickens, and the attendant cannot tell how they are getting on. With a window of reasonable dimensions, however, one can look in quietly at night without even waking the sleepers, or he can observe them by day, and note exactly by their actions as to whether they are all right or otherwise.

Three Chambers Essential.—A foster-mother, except for use indoors, that only consists of one compartment should not be tolerated. Personally, I think three chambers are preferable, one being for sleeping or warming up during the day, the next a little cooler, and the third rather warmer than the outer air. The first and second of these should be glazed in front, and the last protected by a window of fine wire-netting only. A canvas blind or shutter is often useful to prevent driving rain or snow from entering, and if this latter division is open to the ground floor also, so much the better.

The **Lamp** must be given special attention
when choosing a brooder, and, although there
are many kinds in use, some are of better
quality and more reliable than others. The protection which is given the lamp is just about as

Fig. 20.—FOSTER-MOTHERS WITH DETACHABLE RUNS

important, for a flame that is exposed to draughts
will never give a steady heat, and it may be the
means of setting fire to the whole machine. The
means of the disposal of the lamp fumes must
be observed, as well as the method of supplying

the inner compartments with an ample supply of warm air.

The Ventilation is, of course, a most essential point, and, it may be added, very many foster-mothers to-day fail in being too stuffy. Then again, there is the regulation of the ventilation. More fresh air is required for large chickens than for small ones, more on hot days than on cold. There should be no complicated machinery about a foster-mother. The best to-day are the simplest.

Runs.—A small detachable run, as advised for use with coops (Fig. 21), should be provided for each foster-mother for the same reasons already given. Indeed, such a run—which, to a three-compartment foster-mother, constitutes a fourth division—is far more necessary with artificially-hatched chickens than with others. Without the hen to call them the youngsters are easily lost or chilled, if unable to find their way home, when out for the first few days, but after they have spent those days within the protection of the run they may be given fuller liberty with confidence.

Temperature.—Most foster-mothers are provided with thermometers, placed at about the warmest part of the sleeping place, and before the chickens are removed from the "drying-box," or the incubator " nursery," the thermometer should stand at about 90 deg. Rather less will do if the season is late and the weather warm. In transferring from the one place to the other, the same precautions must be taken that have been mentioned before to prevent the chickens taking cold —exposure to severe winds being the most dangerous.

Feeding the Chicks.—The feeding of artificially-hatched chickens may be carried out precisely as already recommended so far as the food is concerned, but the mode of giving it is obviously rather different. In the first instance, as soon as the chickens are settled in the brooder, a little egg food may be sprinkled around the hover, and, if the weather is fine and the birds strong, some may be put in the second chamber to encourage them to run about. Food should not be given in the sleeping place any longer than is necessary—not after the second day. Everything, in fact, should be done to induce the

chickens to come out. Weakness soon follows
continued exposure to a heated atmosphere, and
chickens thus affected do not easily recover—
they are the first for disease to claim. Dry food
is even more useful in the foster-mother than it
is in the coop. It may be sprinkled in the litter
(which may be, as before recommended, dry
earth and chaff for preference) to encourage
scratching exercise and afford diversion; or a
little trough or shallow box of it may be placed
in the foster-mother, so that the chickens can
help themselves when so inclined. When rearing with the natural mother, to put the dry food
in the litter or within reach would mean that
she would eat most of it. And if it were placed
in the open, wild birds and vermin would con-
sume it. When giving any of the soft foods
advised in another chapter they must always be
fed outside on clean turf, or, if the weather be
very bad, in well-scoured troughs placed in the
coolest part of the brooder. The water, too,
must be as far away from the heated chambers
as circumstances will permit. Green food is
even more essential to artificially-hatched
chickens than to others, and the daily supply,
particularly in the early months of the year,

must on no account be omitted. As to the number of meals to be given each day, and the amount of food to be allowed, the feeder must be guided by the chickens' appetites, and other circumstances already discussed.

Temperature and Ventilation.—The regulation of the temperature and ventilation—terms which are not quite synonymous—is a most important matter when rearing artificially. Starting with the foster-mother at 90 deg., it may be reduced to about 85 deg. by the end of the first week. Then a further but gradual reduction may take place until the thermometer in the warmest part stands at 70 deg., the chickens being rather more than a fortnight old. At that it may remain in the early months of the year for some weeks. But rather than rely upon the thermometer, the rearer will do better to accustom himself to judge the temperature by the motions of the chickens themselves. Supposing, to begin with, that the temperature under the hover is comfortably hot to the hand, and the brooder is occupied by a normal number of chickens, all should go well. But the attendant ought not to rest content with that. He must take note of what

the chickens are doing every time he goes round.
If they are scattered evenly over the floor of the
sleeping place at night—or under the hover when
they are quite small—and they are quiet and
peaceful, all is well.   On the other hand, if there
is a continual movement and crowding toward

Fig. 21.—Sectional Brooder with Detachable Runs

the hottest part, more heat is required.   When
the temperature is too high the chickens will be
sleeping away from the chief source of heat,
many of them, perhaps, panting and exhausted.
After the age of three weeks, or rather less, the
lamp heat may be much reduced, more especially
at night, when the chickens are all crowded

together in the one chamber; but all along the
attendant must use his common sense and observation, relying upon those two faculties more
than upon thermometers and written directions.

It may be mentioned, however, that overheating is a far more prevalent mistake than the
reverse, and that it, combined with overcrowding, is responsible for a great part of the
mortality which takes place every year. If the
brooder is allowed to attain a "sweating" heat,
indicated by the litter being damp in the morning and the glass streaming with moisture, there
will soon be trouble (diarrhœa, pneumonia, and
other ills) unless prompt measures are taken to
admit more ventilation at night, and to reduce
the lamp heat also if necessary.

When to Discontinue Artificial Heat.—The age
at which lamp heat may be dispensed with depends upon the time of year. In April and May,
or later, chickens will often do quite well without any artificial heating when four to five weeks
old, whereas it may be necessary to maintain it
for two months in earlier days. Here, again,
one must use his own judgment, and do accordingly as weather and other conditions permit.

But in any case the heat must be withdrawn gradually, and the chickens hardened-off by degrees. During this process it will often be found necessary—in cold, wet days particularly—to have the lamp going with a small flame by day, putting it out after the chickens have settled for the night. The reason for this must be obvious. In the daytime the chickens will be continually backward and forward, only some half-dozen or so, perhaps, being in for a warm-up at a time, which is not enough to keep each other comfortable. At night, however, all are near together, and the brooder, too, is shut up more closely than by day, so that less artificial heat is required.

Cold Brooder.—After the chickens have been accustomed to be without lamp heat entirely for a few days they must be transferred to what is called a "cold brooder" (Fig. 24). This is merely a brooder of much larger size, and having more ventilation, or it is a coop or small house of any kind. Its main features must be spaciousness (without being too big for the number of chickens), airiness, and durability. It must be placed away from where the younger lots of chickens are being reared, for reasons already given, and on fresh ground if possible.· From this stage onward the chickens may be treated just in the same way as those reared with the natural mother.

Management of Brooders.—In concluding this

Fig. 22.—A Sectional Movable Brooder

chapter I would emphasize the great importance of keeping brooders well aired and cleaned. They should stand in sunny places, and have their lids open to expose the interiors to sun and air whenever possible. Not less important is the attention that must be given daily to the lamp. It must be kept properly trimmed and clean, or disasters may occur. To put in print the hundred and one things which a chicken rearer will find to do, even if he goes in for the business in quite a small way, would be impossible. All of us are situated differently, or have our own

Fig. 23.—An Out-Door Brooder in Use

circumstances to contend with. But, as we have said before, the work is not a difficult one if we go about it in a methodical, open-minded way. Instead of being bound down with stock phrases, and our common sense swamped by a super-abundance of science or " rule of thumb," if we took things as we found them, and applied ourselves to work with unlimbered faculties, how much better off we should be! We do not venture to hint that science is out of place in the chicken nursery, nor that books and periodicals

Fig. 24.—A Cold Brooder.

should not be consulted and studied well, but we do say—and say it with emphasis—that most chicken rearers are blind. Their intelligence and faculty of observation have been sacrificed for some "system," some "authority," some new-fangled theory that has been expounded not always with unselfish motives. We know of no class whose hands are so tied, whose faculties are so stunted as those of poultry-keepers. In incubation and rearing the power of the "hen-wife" compared with that of reason is as a mountain to a mole-hill. The belief in the peppercorn and the pip is more revered than the latest achievement of a competition layer by those people whom we want to encourage more than any others. The ideas about the moon affecting the hatching of eggs, the prejudice against incubators, and the silly notions regarding them; the interest still taken in any old fraud who says he or she can foretell sex in eggs —these and many others are still unshaken in country districts. And they are these things, together with the poultry-keepers who will not use their observation and general intelligence which Nature has given them, which are the greatest opposing forces to the progress of poultry culture.

CHAPTER X

REARING IN WINTER

POULTRY farmers who make a speciality of supplying table poultry often have to do much of their rearing in winter, when shelter of some kind beyond that provided by the coop or brooder must be afforded. This shelter may be anything from a few thatched hurdles placed in an orchard or stack-yard, wherein the farmer may rear a brood or so, to an elaborate range of sheds or brooder-house capable of accommodating thousands of chickens at once. That some shelter is essential in the depth of winter is admitted by all who have ever tried to bring up chickens in what may be called such an unnatural time of year, and each one who wishes to undertake the work must lay out his plans according to his requirements or expectations. The specialist who is working a large plant will need no advice from us. He must be an expert himself at the work or he will soon come to grief. The suggestions offered are rather for the guidance of the farmer, the cottager, or the small holder.

Incubator Houses.—Whenever there is a good market for early chickens, and a desire on the part of some one engaged in other agricultural pursuits to supply that market, it will pay to erect a range of lean-to sheds for the protection of the chickens. The work need not be elaborately done, for all that is needed is a good roof and a good floor—the former to throw off rain and the latter to keep the litter perfectly dry, and prevent vermin, such as rats, from entering. Rather than make a winter rearing-shed against a wall, as is often done, with its roof sloping toward the sun, it should be constructed—even if at a little greater expense—the other way about, viz., with its highest part at the front, and the roof sloping to the back. The reason for this is obvious. If the front is higher than the back, and the erection is facing toward the south, all the winter sun will enter. But if it is made the opposite way most of the sun's rays will fall upon the roof. The diagram will explain my meaning more clearly. The glass awning is not essential, but it is a great advantage. But if the glass is not used, some canvas or waterproof sacking blinds must be fixed so that they may be drawn down across the netting at night, or to screen the interior from driving rain or snow by day.

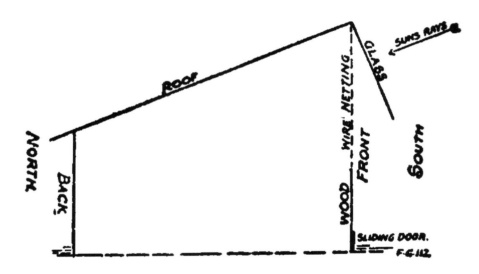

Fig. 25.—Diagram of Shed for Winter Rearing

Foster-Mothers or Coops, may be placed in such a shed, and the former may, if desired, be of a type especially constructed for indoor work. The whole of the shed floor must be well littered with some short material, and it should be divided into sections with wire netting so that the various batches of chickens may be kept separate. Outside the shed there ought to be a good grass run to each inner division, a small sliding door being used to allow the chickens to pass in and out. The advantages of an outside run in winter are very great, and it will be found that there are many days quite mild enough to be enjoyed by the chickens even in December and January. Cold winds, rain, and snow are the elements to be guarded against. A dry cold, such as frost, is not nearly so harmful.

Food for the Chicks.—Of course chickens that are confined to sheds require even more attention than do those outside. They must be supplied with ample fresh green stuff daily, and they must be kept employed by scratching for dry feed buried in the litter. Overcrowding must be carefully avoided, as always. The same foods as before recommended may be given the indoor chickens, but too much of a starchy nature is liable to bring on disease, and care must be taken not to allow foods of highly stimulating properties, except in small quantities.

It is the custom with some rearers to feed the winter chickens by candle-light about nine or ten o'clock each night, so as to break the long fast, believing that they come on better with such attention.   But although the chickens learn wonderfully quick to come to the light and enjoy their supper, the others which are quietly sleeping grow just as well.   It is a good plan to put a little dry feed in a trough overnight, so that the chickens can get it at the first streak of dawn when rearing under any circumstances.

Vermin.—Finally, the indoor rearer must beware of rats and other vermin. These pests are more pressed by hunger in the winter-time, and get uncommonly bold in hard weather. The interiors of coops and brooders must be frequently turned to the light so as to see whether red mites are putting in an appearance, and the broody hens should be afforded every facility for dusting.

Chicken Rearing in Buildings.—Farmers and cottagers not willing or able to go in for specially-made sheds may rear a few broods quite well in vacant buildings, such as barns, so long as they are rat-proof, light, dry, and airy. In many parts of the country, especially in the West, broods of chickens may often be seen in the depth of winter with no other shelter than that provided by the hen and the hedgerow, or, perhaps, the rick-yard. A large proportion of these fall a pray to vermin, but comparatively few to exposure or disease. Hence it would seem that with a little additional care, particularly as to shutting up at night, the system might be extended successfully with some people.

CHAPTER XI

POULTRY AILMENTS

Diseases

THE poultry keeper has no greater enemy to resist, to fight against, than disease. It is his bête noir, ever at his elbow waiting an opportunity to seize upon and destroy his flock. The negligent breeder who feeds and houses his stock badly is usually the first victim, for he has avoided taking those necessary precautions which would have prevented disease from establishing itself. On the other hand, no matter how careful we may be in matters of hygiene, ailments often occur which must be promptly treated if we would prevent an epidemic. To be prepared to meet disease when it comes is to be more than half-way on the way to stamping it out.

Generally speaking, when a bird is found suffering from an infectious disease, it is wisest to kill it at once, burying it in quicklime. If an attempt at curing is decided upon then the utmost precautions must be taken to isolate the sick bird. A warm, dry shed should be fitted up as a hospital. Provide it with several cages in which to put single birds or more, see that it is well ventilated, free from draughts, and that a " medicine chest " is within reach. The latter need not be an expensive article.

Although poultry are subject to an almost interminable list of ailments, with a few common drugs the attendant will be able to combat most of the every-day diseases. I would suggest that he fit up his " chest " with the following : Some Epsom salts, a small bottle each of spirits of camphor, tincture of aconite, tincture of iodine, chlorodyne, terebene, and carbolic acid. An ounce or two of permanganate of potash and sulphate of iron, a chemist's mixture of iron and phosphate of lime, salad oil, turpentine, and an ointment, such as cosmoline or vaseline ; a few half-grain and grain opium pills.

Before going on to describe, as far as space will allow, the causes, symptoms, and treatment of the better known diseases, let me impress upon the poultry keeper, more particularly the beginner, the importance not only of the im-

mediate isolation of sick fowls, but the equal
necessity of at once finding out the cause of the
complaint. Until the origin of the disease is
discovered and rooted out it is hopeless to attempt curative measures. For convenience, the
following ailments are taken in alphabetical
order.

Anæmia.—Poverty of the blood. CAUSES.—
Insufficient green stuff; overcrowding in dark,
damp, ill-ventilated houses; lack of sunshine
and fresh air. SYMPTOMS.—General depression,
paleness of face and comb; extremities cold;
emaciation; ruffled, lustreless plumage; pale,
flabby flesh.

TREATMENT.—Remove the causes that have
given rise to the ailment. Give nourishing food,
fresh air, green vegetable and an iron tonic.

Bronchitis.—Inflammation of the bronchiæ,
viz., the air passages leading to the lungs.
CAUSES.—Draughts; sudden changes of the temperature. SYMPTOMS.—A "rattle" in the
throat; heavy breathing; sometimes cough and
running at the nostrils; expectoration.

TREATMENT.—Keep the bird warm. Administer two or three drops of spirits of camphor in a teaspoonful of glycerine twice daily. Inhalations of steam from hot water containing a few drops of terebene are useful. Feed on soft, warm food, such as oatmeal porridge or rice pudding slightly seasoned with ginger or cayenne.

Bumble-foot.—A hard, corn-like growth upon the ball of the foot. CAUSES.—Confinement on hard ground. In heavy breeds, the flying down from perches that are too high. Predisposition. SYMPTOMS.—Lameness; swelling of the foot.

TREATMENT.—If the corn is hard, pare it with a sharp knife and apply a little acetic acid to the centre daily. Bed the bird on soft, clean hay. If an abscess forms, the place should be lanced, the matter squeezed out, and the wound washed with warm water. After drying apply carbolic oil and **bandage**.

Cholera.—An epidemic diarrhœa. Highly contagious and apparently allied to the cholera morbus of human beings. CAUSES.—Defective hygiene, dampness, impure water or an intermittent water supply; decomposing matter, animal and vegetable, about the runs; contagion—the bacilli being conveyed into healthy birds by the latter picking up food or grass contaminated by the droppings of affected birds. SYMPTOMS.—Loose evacuations of a white or green color; the bird is sleepy and depressed; plumage ruffled; the fluff about the tail wet and matted together; comb dark; there is great thirst throughout; the disease runs its course rapidly, death taking place (usually in stupor) in a few hours. A post-mortem examination discloses a highly inflamed condition of the intestines, mouth contains a sticky substance, throat is purple. Skin under the plumage very dark, and that upon the abdomen green.

TREATMENT.—None recommended. In the event of the disease being very prevalent, Pasteur's vaccine may be used. It is the only treatment that is of any practical use. The disease is so terribly rapid in its progress that the victims are usually too weak for any treatment by the time restoratives are applied. Further, it is so deadly and contagious that every affected bird, while it lives, is a refuge for untold numbers of bacilli which are liable to be transmitted to healthy stock, no matter how much care is exercised. Kill and burn every bird as soon as it shows the first symptom. Remove the non-affected ones to fresh and dry runs, thoroughly disinfecting the old ones. The droppings of diseased birds should be treated with a strong carbolic acid disinfectant. There is no more difficult disease to stamp out than this one, and unless the most exacting means and persistent effort are employed, it will keep on reappearing, perhaps for years afterward.

Catarrh.—The common "cold in the head" to which we ourselves are subject. CAUSES.—Exposure, draughts, damp, sudden changes of temperature, contagion. SYMPTOMS.—Watery discharge from eyes and nostrils; swollen face; ruffled, lustreless plumage; sneezing.

TREATMENT.—Administer one-third of a teaspoonful of Epsom salts in warm water, and three hours afterward give two or three drops of spirits of camphor on a meal pill. Continue to give the latter twice daily. Keep the eyes, nostrils, and mouth well sponged with a warm, weak solution of permanganate of potash and water, drying thoroughly after each operation. Keep the bird warm, and feed on soft, nourishing foods seasoned with cayenne. Although this disease is not a serious one it is, without doubt, contagious, and, if neglected, may lead to roup.

Crop-bound.—An abnormal accumulation of food of a fibrous, husky, or hard nature in the crop. CAUSES.—Careless, irregular feeding, the presence of long, wiry grass or hairs that bind the contents of the crop into a hard lump; irregular water supply. SYMPTOMS.—The bird is listless, and wanders about by itself. Crop very much distended and hard; the breath foul.

TREATMENT.—Dissolve half an ounce of Epsom salts in a pint of warm water, and give the bird one or two teaspoonfuls. Gently knead the crop so as to soften and loosen the contents. The process is a long and tedious one, but with patience the part will become soft. Then administer a little more of the salts (diluted with warm water), and place the bird in a pen. If after two hours the crop is still its original size, and, if anything, harder than it was, it is best to kill the bird. Supposing, however, that it is a valuable specimen, or one that it is particularly desired to save, an operation must be performed. An incision about one inch long is made at the upper part of the crop, and the contents removed with a small silver or bone spoon. When all is clear, wash the interior of the crop with warm water, containing a little permanganate of potash, and stitch together the aperture. Use a fine needle and silken thread. First get the inner skin secured with not less than three stitches, and then do the same with the outer one. Apply a little carbolic oil to the part, and the bird will soon be all right. For a few days feed on bread and 'milk (not too moist), and do not give any water for forty-eight hours.

Diarrhœa.—CAUSES.—Sudden changes in the temperature; injudicious feeding, dampness, sour food. SYMPTOMS.—Watery evacuations. General depression.

TREATMENT.—In mild cases put a little Epsom salts in the drinking water, and then feed on soft food, mixed crumbly with milk, and containing some boiled rice. If the ailment does not disappear with that, give a meal pill containing three drops of spirits of camphor every three hours, and a 1 grain opium pill every night. In the case of diarrhœa with young chickens, individual treatment is scarcely practicable. Put a lump of camphor in their drinking water, keep them scrupulously clean, feed largely on boiled rice (mixed dry with fine oatmeal), and remove the cause of the ailment, which may usually be found in over-heating or injudicious feeding.

Diphtheria.—Often called " roup," " canker," or " ulceration." A highly contagious, dangerous disease. CAUSES.—A bacillus. Birds usually attacked are those that are or have been suffering from roup. Damp, insanitary houses and runs. Uncleanliness and lack of fresh air and sunshine. It spreads rapidly by contagion. SYMPTOMS.—Catarrhal discharge, depression, specks of white, or large yellowish growths in the throat and mouth, or about the eyes. Offensive breath ; the throat a bluish purple color, emaciation ; finally, the diphtheritic membrane forms across the throat suffocating the bird.

TREATMENT.—In the case of ordinary stock it is wisest to kill off every diseased bird, burning the bodies. The malady, however, is amenable to treatment if taken in time, but the greatest care must be exercised in isolating the sick birds, and all utensils, etc., used by them. Further, it is as well to remember that it is by no means un-likely that this terrible disease can be trans-mitted from animals to man. To cure diseased birds put them in a warm room—one with a moist atmosphere preferably. Remove all growths that come away easily, burning them, and the remaining ones paint with the following lotion, viz., carbolic acid, 1 dr.; sulphurous acid solution, 3 drs.; tincture perchloride of iron, 4 drs.; glycerine, 4 drs. Use a small paint brush, and apply a little to the specks twice or thrice daily. Wash the eyes and nostrils frequently with the solution of permanganate of potash, as advised in the case of "catarrh." Administer a chemist's "sore throat mixture" two or three times a day, allowing a medium-sized bird about one-third human adult dose. Feed on soft, nourishing foods, such as bread and milk, custards, or porridge, for the strength of the patient must be kept up at any cost. When the growths disappear, and the bird begins to look brighter, give an iron tonic and a little raw lean meat daily.

Dropsy.—Sometimes occurs both of the crop and the abdomen, but birds so affected are seldom worth curing. SYMPTOMS.—Accumulations of watery matter in the parts mentioned, causing them to "bag" or become pendulous.

TREATMENT.—Get a veterinary surgeon to

tap the bird. Administer 4 grains of iodide of potassium daily. The crop may be emptied by holding the bird by the legs and causing the liquid to be vomited, by a gentle downward pressure.

Egg-bound.—Inability to eject an egg, usually through the latter being unusually large. Hens that are too fat are frequently egg-bound. SYMPTOMS.—The bird visits the nest frequently, but without laying. The tail is carried low, sometimes touching the ground. The wings droop, and there is evident pain and distress.

TREATMENT.—Foment the vent by holding it over the steam arising from a jug of boiling water for about ten minutes. Lubricate the part with the finger, or a feather dipped in salad oil. Then place the hen in a basket lined with hay, and she will probably pass the egg in a short time. If not, the egg may be assisted toward the aperture by a gentle pressure from the outside, but the greatest care must be exercised to avoid a breakage. Give nearly half a teaspoonful of Epsom salts in a little warm water before commencing operations and again twelve hours afterward.

Egg-eating.—Although scarcely a disease, this bad habit may be treated as one, for when an individual commences egg-eating the vice quickly spreads through the flock like a plague. CAUSES. —Lack of employment, want of shell-making material; empty drinking vessels, broken eggs; too close confinement.

TREATMENT.—Remove the causes and isolate the offenders, giving them a surfeit of egg-shells, bad eggs, or stale ones, morning, noon, and night until the appetite is sickened. If the vice is general, the whole flock may be so treated, using the while patent nests to ensure the safety of the eggs laid. When the vice is cured, give a little sulphur in the soft food every other day for a week.

Eggs, Blood Spots in.—Brought about by slight hæmorrhage in the ovary or oviduct. CAUSES. —Too much stimulating food, such as spices and meat.

TREATMENT.—Give occasional small doses of Epsom salts, and reduce the diet.

Enteritis.—Inflammation of the smaller intestines. An epidemic disease that probably causes the deaths of as many fowls and pheasants every year as do all the other diseases put together. CAUSES.—Ordinary cases of enteritis sometimes occur from fowls eating unslaked lime, poison, or some other irritant, but these are isolated instances compared to an outbreak of contagious enteritis, which is caused by a bacillus that exists in the blood and tissues of diseased fowls and in their evacuations. As in the case of cholera—to which this disease has some resemblance—healthy birds picking up food or grass fouled by the excrement of affected birds contract the disease. SYMPTOMS.—Rapid prostration; heavy breathing; ruffled plumage, diarrhœa, the excrement being yellow or mustard color instead of green as in cholera. The droppings in extreme cases are tinged with blood. There is intense thirst; weakness of the legs and spasmodic shivering.

TREATMENT.—None recommended, but where great issues are at stake, Dr. Klein's vaccine may be resorted to, with the object of checking the progress of the disease. All birds, on showing the first symptoms, should be killed and burned. Remove the non-affected ones to fresh ground, provide ample, dry shelter, and see that the water supply is good and sufficient.

Favus.—A disease caused by a microscopic fungus of a vegetable nature. It first appears as white scabs on the comb or face, which multiply, grow together, and become yellower and thicker if not attended to. The skin of the neck and rump is sometimes invaded, the feathers falling off.

TREATMENT.—Wash the parts with vinegar or warm water and soft soap, then rub in an ointment made of red oxide of mercury one part, and lard six parts. Nitrate of silver may also be applied effectually. Give the bird nourishing food, plenty of green stuff, fresh air, and an iron tonic. In treating the patient it is as well to bear in mind that the spores of the fungus float away in the air like dust, and, settling upon any scratched or abraded skin, take root. Most domestic animals may become affected by the disease in that way, and even man himself is not immune. Many people, therefore, would prefer to kill a diseased bird outright, rather than run the risks that accompany any treatment of this loathsome disease.

Feather-eating.—A vice common to fowls kept in close confinement. It is the result of bad management; overstimulation; lack of exercise and diversion; want of green food; insect pests.

TREATMENT.—Remove the causes which brought it about. Isolate the offenders, and give flowers of sulphur in the soft food (a teaspoonful to every six hens) every other day for a week or more. It is not the slightest use applying any nauseous dressing to the plumage until the cause which developed the vice has been removed.

Gapes.—A disease mainly confined to young chickens, young pheasants, and various species of wild birds. It is caused by the presence of small blood-red worms in the windpipe, which set up irritation, or multiply to such an extent that the bird is suffocated. SYMPTOMS.—Gaping, sneezing, or coughing. Rapid emaciation. The wings droop, and the sufferer often falls backward in its attempts to breathe.

TREATMENT.—The disease is a difficult one to cure on account of the fact that it attacks such young birds, and, usually, so many of them, for when it does break out, it is in the nature of an epidemic. Individuals may be treated in one of the following ways: (a) Strip a feather of its web excepting the tip. Dip it in eucalyptus oil, and pass it down the chicken's windpipe (the entrance to which will be seen at the top of the throat just behind the tongue). Twist it round and withdraw it, and some of the crimson worms, or particles of them, will be seen adhering. To extract all the parasites, the operation will have to be performed several times, exercising great care not to lacerate the windpipe. (b) Take a hot cinder from the fire and pour upon it some carbolic acid. Hold the chicken's head in the fumes that rise up until the bird shows signs of fainting, then immediately place it in the open air to recover. Care must be taken not to overdo the operation by poisoning the patient. (c) When a large number of chickens are attacked they may be put in a fumigating box, and treated with the fumes of carbolic acid en masse. The box must have a perforated false bottom on which the birds must be placed. The carbolic acid must be burned underneath and the box made air-tight at the top. A large pane of glass should be fixed into the lid, so that the operator can observe the chickens within, and immediately expose them to fresh air when they show signs of drooping. The operation will, perhaps, have to be gone through every day for several days before all the birds are cured.

PREVENTION.—All diseases ought, of course, to be prevented as far as possible, but gapes particularly calls for attention in this respect. Always rear chickens on fresh ground if possible. Dampness and humidity are favorable to the ova of the gape worm, which exist in water and in moist earth, so that dry places should be chosen for the chickens. Clean drinking water is essential, and, if gapes is suspected, keep a lump of camphor in each drinking vessel. Give chopped onion or garlic with at least two of the feeds each day. Always burn birds that die of gapes. Keep the chickens robust and free of insect pests ; particularly ticks.

Gout.—A swollen, heated condition of the feet and joints, usually attacking birds that are brought up in close confinement, and which are unsuitably fed.

TREATMENT.—Dissolve Epsom salts in the drinking water, give a plain diet, and plenty of green stuff. To relieve the affected parts immerse them in warm water, afterward applying a liniment.

Leg-weakness.—Young, growing cockerels of the heavy breeds often lose the use of their legs at the age of five or six months, especially if they have been forced. It is best to kill such birds, as they will be of no use for breeding, unless required for show purposes.

TREATMENT.—Nutritious but non-fattening food. Administer one-third adult human being doses of a salts of iron and phosphate of lime mixture. Rub the legs with an embrocation if cramp sets in. The use of dry bone meal from an early age will go far to prevent leg-weakness.

Liver Disease (Tuberculosis).—One of the commonest and most dreaded of all poultry diseases. CAUSES.—A tuberculous bacillus, considered by many to be analogous to that which attacks mammalian animals. When the bacilli are found in the lungs the disease is known as "consumption." Highly contagious, and if the disease itself is not actually inherited, the tendency to it undoubtedly is. Poultry suffering from liver disease should not be bred from, they are unfit for food, and it would be very unwise to eat eggs laid by them. Birds that are overfed and kept in ill-ventilated houses and dirty runs are most liable to **attack**. SYMPTOMS.—Emaciation ("going light"), particularly of the breast flesh, lameness, appetite variable, but often quite good; comb and wattles pale; a yellowish tint about the face; sunken, dull eyes. A post-mortem examination discloses cheesy growths upon the liver and often extending to the other organs.

TREATMENT.—None recommended. Kill and burn all diseased birds, and remove the others from the infected area; thoroughly cleansing and disinfecting the latter, and leaving it vacant for at least twelve months. Pay special attention to ventilation (oxygen being known to be the greatest enemy of the tuberculous bacillus), and to cleanliness; feed on a non-stimulating diet, giving plenty of fresh green stuff daily as well as grit and pure water.

Pneumonia.—Inflammation of the lungs. CAUSES.—Sudden changes of temperature, exposure, and, in young chickens (especially those reared in foster-mothers), overcrowding, and consequent overheating, at night. Hereditary predisposition. SYMPTOMS.—Cough, gasping for breath; expectoration; ruffled plumage; a crackling sound can be heard if the ear is placed against the bird's back between the shoulders.

TREATMENT. In the ease of adults paint the skin on the back between the wings with iodine once daily. Give three drops of chlorodyne in a teaspoonful of linseed tea every four hours until improvement sets in, when it may be given less frequently. Keep the bird warm and feed on a soft, nutritious diet. Little can be done to relieve young chickens. Give more room and fresh air at night, and mix a few drops of chlorodyne and a teaspoonful of glycerine in each half-pint of drinking water.

Rheumatism.—Distinguished from gout by the absence of swelling and heat. CAUSES.—Dampness, cold; many birds are hereditarily predisposed to rheumatism.

TREATMENT.—Rub the parts with any good liniment—one of chloroform and belladonna being exceptionally serviceable. Keep the bird warm, and give a mild aperient, such as a small dose of Epsom salts once daily. Feed on an unstimulating diet, in which has been mixed a pinch each of bicarbonate of soda and chlorate of potash.

Roup.—A highly contagious form of catarrh, sometimes becoming malignant or diphtheritic (see Diphtheria). CAUSES.—Insanitation, draughts, overcrowding, dampness, cold, contagion. SYMPTOMS.—The disease usually commencing as a common cold (see "Catarrh") it must be treated as such, but when there is a thickening of the discharge from nostrils and eyes, and the breath becomes very foul, other measures should be resorted to. A bird affected by roup is feverish and depressed. The face swells so that the eyes are often entirely hidden and sealed up; breathing is labored, emaciation rapid.

TREATMENT.—Sponge the parts continually, as advised under "Catarrh." Give eight drops of sal volatile in a teaspoonful of warm water twice daily, and paint the swollen parts with iodine, taking care that the tincture does not get into the bird's eyes. As soon as improvement sets in give a mineral tonic in one-third human adult doses. Keep the bird warm, and feed on a nourishing diet, such as bread and milk, or porridge, seasoned with a little cayenne or ginger. Thoroughly clean and disinfect the runs and houses that contained the diseased birds; find out the cause of the outbreak and remove it.

Scaly Leg.—See page 145.

Tuberculosis.—See "Liver Disease."

White Comb.—Birds that are kept in dark, damp, ill-ventilated runs, deprived of green food and sunlight, contract a mild disease of the comb, upon which appears a white scurf or powdering, which sometimes extends to the feathers of the neck and body.

TREATMENT.—Remove the causes of the disease, and mix a little sulphur in the soft food every alternate day for a week. Supply a plentiful allowance of green stuff, nourishing, non-heating food, and give (after discontinuing the sulphur) a mineral tonic. Carbolic oil may be applied to the affected parts.

Worms.—Birds suffering from parasitical worms in the intestines are listless, weak, and thin, although they may eat well—sometimes ravenously. These symptoms being, however, common to other diseases, the droppings underneath the perches should be examined for traces of worms. If the latter are the cause of the ailment, they will be discovered whole, or in pieces, in the evacuations.

T<small>REATMENT</small>.—Administer one **grain of san-
tonin** and five grains of powdered areca nut in a
tablespoonful of warm milk and water to each
affected bird. Give the dose when the bird is
fasting, and feed on warm, soft food for a day or
two. Fowls that are kept in dirty runs and fed
on impure food and unsound grain are most subject to worms.

Vermin

Lice.—If provided with a good dust bath,
healthy fowls will usually rid themselves of
these pests, but when only a few are kept it
is desirable to dust them individually with
pyrethrum powder. Old stock cocks and broody
hens particularly require individual attention.
To dust a fowl properly she should be held by
the legs by an attendant and laid on a news-
paper. The operator can then raise the feathers
with one hand while he uses the dredger with
the other. The powder must be got well under
the feathers, and that which falls off, and which
would otherwise be lost, may be gathered up off
the paper. An oil made up of linseed oil eight
parts, and paraffin two parts, may be used by
applying it in small quantities on different parts

of the body, more particularly at the root of the tail and under the wings. Where a number of fowls are kept, I am in favor of submitting them to an annual dip, to take place in July or August. The dip may be prepared as follows :—Dissolve, by boiling, one pound of any well-known disinfectant soap, and one pound of yellow soap in three quarts of water. When boiling add a pint of paraffin (precaution being taken against fire), and a tablespoonful of carbolic acid; mix this thoroughly and dilute with sixteen quarts of water. Choose a warm day for the operation, and dip each fowl for about two minutes, working the water well into the feathers. Rinse in a tub of plain water and, after squeezing as much water as possible out of the feathers, the fowl may be held by the legs to flap her wings and then replaced in the run. The dip is used cold and no injurious effects follow.

Fleas are often troublesome during the summer months, and infest the houses and nests more than they do the hens themselves. If not checked they increase with amazing rapidity, and I have seen them so numerous that the poultryman refused to enter the houses to collect the eggs!

Frequent lime-washing is an effectual preventive of all insect pests, but when once the vermin have taken possession of a house, more stringent measures will have to be employed. Pyrethrum may be used in the nests, but spraying with a very fine spray-pump, using the above dip diluted with only two quarts of water, is far more deadly. This must be done at intervals during the summer, or whenever the insects show signs of their presence.

The Red Mite is a very minute creature, making its home in the cracks and crevices of perches and walls, and coming out at night to suck the fowls' blood. The ravages of these pests have often been the main cause of failures in poultry keeping; they increase rapidly, and literally swarm in thousands if not instantly prevented, and hens that are not only tormented but weakened by loss of blood can scarcely be expected to lay. The mites may be killed by the application of paraffin, or by spraying, as recommended above. Whatever method be employed, the perches particularly must be dressed with the liquid as well as the slots in which they rest. Attending to the perches in this way will also prevent the spread of the species of itch-mite which is the cause of the loathsome disease known as

Scaly Leg.—Those breeds of fowls that have feathered shanks are more liable to attack from this parasite. The legs and feet become scurfy, and a dirty white color. An encrustation forms, the scales of the leg become detached and fall off, and the bird frequently loses the entire use of its limbs. Diseased fowls should have their legs and feet scrubbed with a nail-brush, and an emulsion of soft soap and warm water, afterward being dressed with a solution of paraffin and lard, in equal parts, and thoroughly mixed when warm. The operation may have to be repeated several times, but the great thing is to check the disease before it has made much progress.

CHAPTER XII

PRESERVING EGGS

I AM not an advocate for preserving eggs for marketing purposes unless there are uncommon circumstances to justify one's doing it. Preserved eggs, however, come in very useful for the household during the winter months, and either one or other of the following methods of preserving may be employed. It is of the greatest importance that all eggs intended to be kept for any length of time be quite fresh when placed in the preservative.

Water-Glass.—To one pound of water-glass, which almost any druggist will supply, add six quarts of hot water. Stir briskly and leave to cool, then pour the liquid into the vessel, which may be of almost any material, and place the latter in a cool place. The eggs may then be put in daily, as they are laid, until the vessel is nearly full, but at least an inch of liquid should remain above the eggs.

Lime.—Pour 1 gallon of water on to 1 lb. of

quicklime. The following day stir the mixture and add 6 ozs. of salt and 1 oz. of cream of tartar, mixing the whole well together. When all the sediment has settled, place the eggs in an earthen-

Fig. 26.—Coop for Broody Hens

ware jar and pour over them the clear liquid. Eggs may be put in from day to day, but they must always be well covered. Before boiling preserved eggs, the larger end should be pierced with a pin.

How To Treat Broody Hens

The old-fashioned methods of "curing" a hen of her broodiness, either by ducking her in a pond or putting her in a dark place to starve for three or four days, have been superseded by the more humane and more effective broody coops. A box, three feet six inches long, and three feet wide may easily be made into a broody coop for six hens, as follows: Waterproof the top, and nail round bars two inches apart at the bottom, running lengthwise. Construct the front as in the illustration, and place a trough for food and a pan for water within reach of the prisoners. The hens only being able to perch on the bars, there is a continual passage of cool air underneath them, when the coop is placed on legs, which soon cures them of the broody instinct. During the process, which usually lasts about three days, they must be regularly fed and watered, so that they will soon be able to commence laying again, and if the coop is placed in sight of the other fowls, so much the better.

Tables For Poultry Keepers
Periods of Incubation

Hen	20 to 22 days	Turkey	28 to 30 days.
Duck	28 to 30 "	Guinea Fowl	26 to 28 "
Goose	28 to 31 "	Pea Fowl	28 to 30 "

MATING POULTRY

Ducks, Heavy Breeds	...	2 or 3 to 1 drake.
" Light "	...	3 or 4 to 1 "
Hens, Heavy "	...	5 to 7 to 1 cock.
" Light "	...	6 to 8 to 1 "
Geese	...	2 or 3 to 1 gander.
Turkeys	...	5 to 8 to 1 cock.

In mating, it must always be borne in mind that the males differ considerably in constitutional vigor, and some may be more heavily mated than others. Male birds on unlimited runs may be given nearly twice as many hens as would suffice in confinement.

TABLE OF FOODS

There is in every 100 parts by weight of—	Flesh-forming Material viz., Gluten, etc.	Warmth-giving and Fattening Material.		Bone-Making Material or Mineral Substances.	Husk or Fibre.	Water.
		Fat or Oil.	Starch.			
Beans and Peas ...	25	2	48	2	8	15
Oatmeal	18	6	63	2	2	9
Middlings, Thirds, or Fine Sharps	18	6	53	5	4	14
Oats	15	6	47	2	20	10
Wheat	12	3	70	2	1	12
Buckwheat ...	12	6	58	1½	11	11½
Barley	11	2	60	2	14	11
Indian Corn ...	11	8	65	1	5	10
Hempseed ...	10	21	45	2	14	8
Rice	7	a trace	80	a trace	—	13
Potatoes	6½	—	41	2	—	50½
Milk	4½	3	5	¾	—	86¾

CHAPTER XIII

THE POULTRY KEEPER'S CALENDAR

January.—The first month of the year is a most important one for the poultry keeper. The main business is the mating of the breeding-pens, upon which so much depends. Go carefully over each bird, rejecting all those that are undersized, diseased, malformed, or which do not promise to fulfil the object in view. See that the cock or cockerel has been well-fed and is in prime condition. If he does not mate readily, but bullies the hens, replace him by another. Do not overstock the pens, but endeavor to allow as much liberty as possible. Provide plenty of litter in the houses and sheds, and keep the birds busy scratching for some hidden corn when the weather is too bad for them to get outside. Give the breeders a good proportion of nitrogenous food such as cut-bone, meat or pea meal, and, if the weather is severe, allow some maize occasionally. Hatch as many chicks for the table-fowl trade as possible. They will fetch top

150

prices at Easter, and later, and will well repay the owner for the extra attention required. Provide plenty of shelter for both young and old, and keep all as dry as possible. See that the breeding stock are not too young. A cockerel mated to two-year-old hens, or an old, but vigorous, " rooster " mated with pullets, will produce the strongest chickens.

February.—Hatching chickens for table must still be continued vigorously. The demand for eggs for incubation will increase this month, and to satisfy your customers as well as yourself, the germs must be kept strong. The stock birds must not be neglected for the sake of the youngsters. Maintain the former in a good, vigorous condition, without overstimulating the egg-organs nor overfeeding. Grit and shell, or old mortar rubbish, are absolutely essential materials for the maintenance of robust health. Do not overdo the moisture in the incubators, and the nest of the sitting hen will require none at all. This is proverbially a month of rain, and few things are more productive of disease than sloppy ground, and wet, foul sleeping places. Collect eggs frequently, and store until required, in a cool, dry place. If placed large end downward, in boxes and covered with bran, so much the better. Be careful that the older chickens are not overcrowded at night, and go round the foster-mothers after dark to see that all is well. Remember that the sun rises earlier every day, and the stock must not be kept waiting for breakfast. Feed the youngest first.

March.—If the breeds kept are of the heavier kinds—Orpingtons, Wyandottes, or Asiatic cross-breds—the main supply of pullets for the following winter's laying must now be hatched. Set every available egg throughout this month, for " there's no chicken like a March chicken." Do not confine the menu to any particular method of feeding. Ring the changes between the various meals, and use soft mixtures and "dry feed " alternately. Watch the chickens' appetites, and feed accordingly ; the oftener the better so long as they are always keen and eat hungrily. Animal food as well as fresh vegetable is necessary, and full advantage must be taken of every gleam of sunshine. The older chickens will benefit by having at least one feed a day of boiled barley. Let them have as much liberty as possible. Some linseed meal added to the staple mixture of ground oats and middlings will assist feathering, and green cut-bone will give them stamina, and increase the rapidity of growth. Keep an eye on the breeding-pens and, if one or more of the stock cocks appears to be going off in condition, immediately put him by himself and feed him up. If there is one held in reserve in case of such an emergency so much the better. Cod-liver oil and quinine capsules are useful in such cases.

April.—Hatching the heavier breeds may still be continued if the last month's output proved inadequate. The non-sitting varieties—Anconas, Leghorns, and Minorcas—must be produced this month, so that they will begin to lay before winter sets in. They mature faster than the Asiatics and are, on the whole, more profitable as egg producers. There are probably more chickens hatched in April than in any other month, and overcrowding must be avoided at all cost. As the foster-mothers become vacated by the older lots, wash them out with quicklime containing a little paraffin oil, and lean them open to the sun and air. Keep old and young separate, and put the cockerels and pullets of the earlier hatches apart as soon as they can be distinguished. Put the "best" on the market at the first opportunity, but beware of sending out undersized, badly fattened specimens. Aim at the "best," and grade the consignments according to size and quality. If there are any surplus eggs, incubate them, and sell the chicks as "day-olds," or place the former in a preservative. They must, however, be fresh when put in the latter, no matter what it may be composed of.

May.—Sittings of eggs from the lighter breeds may still be advertised, and the last batches of chickens from such must be brought off before the end of the month. Those country poultry keepers who cater for a seaside trade must commence hatching eggs for table fowl and ducklings. There will be a brisk demand for the latter in most places during the "season." Add some dry bone-meal to the food prepared for pullets and cockerels which are to be kept for stock. Now that the sun is gaining power less artificial heat will be required during the daytime in the brooders. Give the eggs in the incubators rather more airing and allow the broody hens fifteen to twenty minutes daily. Do not forget to use insect powder freely in the nests and see that the dust baths are dry. A sprinkling of powdered sulphur over the latter will be beneficial.

June.—Long days and short nights, much work and little rest, are the lot of the poultry keeper this month. Expenses are also high on account of the number of young stock on hand. Late broods of chickens or lots from the incubator that are not required, should be disposed of. The insect fiend must be vigorously attacked this month. Examine the youngest chickens for ticks, and the older ones for lice, every few days. Ticks will be found adhering to the skull and neck, and must be killed by the application of a drop or two of carbolized oil (1 in 20). Insect powder will destroy the lice ; and the litter in the coops and foster-mothers must be frequently renewed. Keep a sharp lookout for the " red mite " (see Chapter XI), and exterminate it before it becomes established, or there will be untold trouble. Now that vegetable food is becoming plentiful, it will simplify the work to use " dry feed " very largely. Provide plenty of fresh water daily. Break up the breeding pens and dispose of all those old hens or pullets that have laid during the past year, and which will be no longer required. The stock cocks which are to be kept on may be put into the cockerel pens. Give the growing pullets as much liberty as possible, and run them in movable houses in the open fields if possible.

July.—The work for this month will be, for the most part, a repetition of that of June. It is still needful to maintain a sharp lookout for vermin, and to avoid overcrowding, both by day and night. Provide ample shade from the hot sun, and keep the drinking water cool.

August.—The trade at the seaside or other holiday resorts will now be at its height. It will not last many weeks so that the poultry keeper who is prepared for it will come off best. Some of the earlier pullets will be commencing to lay. Do not force them nor spoil your market by putting their immature eggs in with the larger ones. Do not allow pullets and old hens to run together.

September.—The process of weeding out the stock may now be commenced, and it will be necessary, on account of the differences in size, to continue it for some months. Cockerels and pullets must not only be kept apart, but those intended for stock and those destined for table must be separated. Give the moulting birds a little powdered sulphur in the soft food : it will assist feather growth. Set eggs of good quality table fowls, and large ducks, to produce youngsters to be ready for the Christmas market. Lay in a good stock of peat moss or collect the autumn leaves, storing in a dry place for winter littering. If the demand for goslings is good, dispose of as many as possible this month and next.

October.—Commence feeding the pullets more generously, giving animal food (cut green-bone, if possible) daily. If there is any stubble let them have full advantage of it. Keep the birds in small flocks—fifteen to twenty. Look out for leg-weakness among the cockerels of the heavier breeds. Dry bone-meal may still be used, and a piece of sulphate of iron, the size of a filbert, placed in each quart of water. Give all coops and foster-mothers a thorough cleaning before putting them away.

November.—The pullets will require special

attention this month as regards feeding. Continue the meat or green-bone and allow some maize occasionally in the afternoons. Keep the houses dry and well littered, and encourage scratching exercise under cover in bad weather. Remember that dampness retards egg-production, and the layers must be kept comfortable without being coddled. Some pea or bean meal will be a useful addition to the staple diet, and linseed meal is also highly beneficial in cold, damp weather. The autumn chickens and ducklings must be given ample vegetable and animal food, and a dry, well-littered shelter is no less important for them than it is in the case of the layers. Feed well on a somewhat fattening diet, house well, and limit the range, so that the birds will not be so much affected by the closer confinement necessary during the last stages of fattening. Get your Christmas orders in good time.

December.—Pen the Christmas ducks, turkeys, and geese, and increase the " fatty " constituents of the daily fare. Cage-fed fowls may now be crammed for those markets which appreciate and pay for the extra weight and quality. Use skim milk (or buttermilk) and ground oats largely for fattening all classes of poultry.   Aim at producing the very best.   Put the stock on the market properly packed, clean, and graded.

Balance the account of receipts and expenditure at the end of every month, and again every six months, *i. e.,* in June and December.   Keep a careful record of the stock, both " live " and " dead," and bear in mind that success cannot be attained without accurate bookkeeping.

Made in the USA
San Bernardino, CA
11 February 2017